THE DIGITAL WORLD PLAYBOOK

Master The Digital AI shift, Understand Future Trends, and Build Lasting Wealth in The New Economy

By Sterlyn Markell Smith

Copyright Page

THE DIGITAL WORLD PLAYBOOK (Master The Digital AI Shift, Future Trends, and Building Lasting Wealth in The New Economy)

For permission requests, contact:
[sterlyns@yahoo.com]

ISBN: 978-17352942-7-8
Publisher: [Sterlyn Smith]
Cover Design: [Sterlyn Smith]
Interior Layout: [Sterlyn Smith]
Editing: [Sterlyn Smith]

Disclaimer:
The information in this book is provided for educational and inspirational purposes only. The author and publisher are not liable for any actions taken based on the content of this book.

Printed in [USA]
First Edition: [December, 2025]

Dedication

This book is dedicated to the digital visionaries, business builders, and those individuals seeking of a better future.

To the Entrepreneur. You are the engine of the new economy, and this playbook is your fuel.

To the employee who feels the ground shifting, who senses the power of AI and economic uncertainty and refuses to be a spectator. If you are someone proactively preparing and arming yourself with the skills to not just survive, but to thrive in the digital shift. Your courage to learn and adapt is the first pillar of success.

To the individual who has felt locked out of the secrets of wealth, for whom money felt like a complex code and credit score a perpetual barrier. This is your key. Taking ownership of your financial destiny is the most powerful negotiation you will ever close.

I dedicate this work to my family and friends whose unwavering support was the focus that converted my scattered ideas into a carefully planned mission. You are my most valuable asset.

To the mentors and guides who illuminated the path, teaching me the critical difference between a creative mind that builds the future and an educated mind that simply memorizes the past. Your lessons on the habits of success and the psychology of the customer are woven into every chapter.

And to you, the reader. You have chosen to invest in your most valuable asset: your mind. You are here to decipher the trends, master the digital tools, and build something that lasts. You are seeking not just information, but transformation, from understanding the power and the future of e-commerce, to cultivating the millionaire habits that lead to lasting wealth.

The journey ahead requires more than just knowledge; it demands an unshakable mindset, the resilience to overcome post-pandemic challenges, and the skill to turn a first-time buyer into a customer for life.

This playbook is my commitment to your journey. It is a map through the digital wilderness, a shield against economic storms, and a blueprint for building a legacy of prosperity and freedom.

Acknowledgements

It is with a heart full of gratitude that I take this moment to acknowledge those who made *The Digital World Playbook* possible.

First and foremost, I bow my head in humble gratitude to God. Thank you for blessing me with a curious and analytical mind, one that questions the status quo, thinks deeply about the rapid currents of change, and seeks to discern true, lasting value amidst the noise of the present moment. This is a divine gift, has been the foundation upon which this book is built.

My profound love and thanks go to my parents. To my mother and father, you nurtured and raised me not just to succeed, but to be a thoughtful and creative person, encouraging me to see the world not just as it is, but as it could be. The values you instilled in me, integrity, perseverance, and the courage to think differently, are written into the fabric of every page. I am the person I am today because of your unwavering love and guidance.

To my son, you are my greatest motivation and my most powerful inspiration. You are the reason I look toward the future with both hope and determination. The desire to build a better world for you, to model resilience, and to become the very best version of myself pushes me to strive for more each day.

I am also deeply indebted to my extended family and my circle of friends. Thank you for your steadfast support throughout my entire life. To those who stood by me, celebrated my victories, and, most importantly, lifted me in prayer during the many challenging and uncertain times.

Finally, I wish to acknowledge you, the reader. By choosing this book, you have taken a decisive step toward understanding and mastering the future. Your quest for knowledge is what gives this work its ultimate purpose. I am honored to be a part of your journey.

With deepest thanks,

Sterlyn Smith

Introduction

Welcome to

The Digital World Playbook

Master The Digital AI shift, Understand Future Trends, and Build Lasting Wealth in The New Economy

If you're holding this book, you recognize that the digital landscape is not just changing; it is undergoing a huge shift, powered by Artificial Intelligence. This isn't about merely having an online presence, it's about fundamentally re-engineering how you think, operate, and create value in an AI-driven world.

Within these pages, we provide more than just inspiration; we deliver a concrete blueprint. You will learn to harness cutting-edge technologies, decipher emerging trends, and implement the financial and psychological strategies that separate transient success from generational wealth. If you are ready to move from being a passive participant to an active creator of your financial future, you are in the right place.

The Four Pillars of a Future-Proof Business

This book is structured around four core pillars, each essential for building a resilient and thriving enterprise in the new economy. We will deconstruct each one, providing you with actionable frameworks and insights.

Pillar 1: Mastering The AI Universe

Move beyond the hype and learn to leverage AI as your most powerful co-pilot. We will demystify how AI can automate routine tasks, generate creative content, personalize customer experiences at scale, and provide data-driven insights that were once the domain of Fortune 500 companies.

- **What you'll learn:** The difference between predictive and generative AI, prompt engineering basics, and how to integrate AI tools into your core workflows without replacing your unique human touch.
- **Key Resource: (https://www.futuretools.io)**– A constantly updated collection of the best and newest AI tools, categorized by use case.

Pillar 2: Financial Fortitude: The Bedrock of Wealth
Wealth in the new economy isn't just about revenue; it's about intelligent financial architecture. This section moves beyond basic budgeting to teach you the principles of building a solid financial foundation that can withstand economic volatility.

- **What you'll learn:** Strategies for managing and eliminating debt, restructuring your spending to fund investments, and the fundamentals of investing in digital assets and the broader market. You will adopt the "scarcity-to-abundance" mindset that allows the wealthy to grow their capital continuously.
- **Key Resource: (https://investopedia.com)**– An invaluable encyclopedia for financial terms and concepts. Use it to understand everything from **"compound interest"** to **"tokenization."**

Pillar 3: The Empowered Entrepreneur's Toolkit
Your success is accelerated by the tools you use. We will explore the essential software and platforms that empower small businesses to compete with giants. This includes everything from CRM and email marketing platforms to AI-powered analytics and project management tools.

- **What you'll learn:** How to build a "tech stack" that works for you, the power of automated email marketing funnels, and how to create high-converting landing pages that turn visitors into customers.
- **Key Resource: Product Hunt** – A fantastic platform to discover new and innovative business software and apps as they launch.

Pillar 4: Decoding the Future: Trends for Sustainable Growth
The future belongs to those who can see it coming. We analyze the most critical emerging trends in e-commerce, consumer behavior, and digital communication. Understanding these shifts allows you to pivot proactively, not reactively.

- **What you'll learn:** The rise of hyper-personalization, the impact of voice search and visual commerce, and the growing importance of community-driven branding. You'll learn not just to follow trends, but to anticipate them.
- **Key Resource**:**(https://www.trendwatching.com)**– A leading firm in trend analysis, offering insightful reports on consumer trends that are shaping the global market.

Your Journey: From Adversity to Architecture

Every entrepreneur's path is punctuated with tests and challenges. Economic uncertainty, market saturation, and personal setbacks can easily derail your progress. This book was written with that reality in mind. It is your guide to not only surviving these challenges but using them as fuel for growth.

You will gain practical knowledge on a wide range of critical topics, including:

- **Building Resilience:** Preparing your business for economic shifts and building a model that is antifragile.
- **The Entrepreneur's Mindset:** Unpacking the 8 psychological pillars that underpin lasting success.
- **The Art of the Deal:** Mastering negotiation skills that secure favorable terms and close sales.
- **Modern Marketing Mastery:** From the fundamentals of affiliate marketing to the advanced science of crafting landing pages that convert.
- **E-Commerce Excellence:** Understanding the full customer journey, from first click to lifelong loyalty, and how to get customers to buy from you repeatedly.
- **Financial Fluency:** Learning the secrets of how money truly works and taking ownership of your financial identity, including your credit score.
- **Habits of High Achievers:** Integrating 10 invaluable millionaire success habits into your daily routine.
- **Strategic Thinking:** Understanding the powerful difference between a creative mind (which generates possibilities) and an educated mind (which executes on them).

Your Call to Action

The Digital World Playbook is designed for action. The concepts are broken down into digestible, practical steps that you can immediately apply to overcome the obstacles holding you back. The resources provided are timely and relevant, offering pathways for deeper education and real implementation.

Upon completing this book, you will not just have knowledge; you will have a clear, actionable plan. You will be equipped to stop dreaming about the business and life you want and start creating it.

Don't wait for the future to happen to you. Start building it today. Welcome to your new blueprint.

Table of Contents

Section 1
How To Profit with The Power of Artificial Intelligence (AI)

Chapter 1

THE AI-EMPOWERED PROFESSIONAL LEADER

A Manager's Guide to Harnessing Generative AI, Inspiring Teams, and Mitigating Risk

Chapter Introduction:

The AI revolution is not a distant future; it's reshaping the business landscape today. As a manager, you are the critical link between the strategic potential of AI and the people who will bring it to life. This chapter moves beyond the hype to provide you with a practical, non-technical framework for becoming an AI-empowered leader. You will learn how to demystify the technology for your team, leverage its transformative power to gain a competitive edge, and build a culture of responsible and enthusiastic adoption.

What You Will Achieve in This Chapter

By the end of this chapter, you will be equipped to:

- **Lead with Knowledge:** Speak confidently about AI and Generative AI without needing a background in coding or data science.
- **Identify & Leverage Opportunities:** Pinpoint high-impact areas within your team or department where AI can drive efficiency, creativity, and growth.
- **Build an AI-Positive Culture:** Proactively address and alleviate employee fears, turning anxiety into excitement and engagement.
- **Navigate the Risks:** Understand, evaluate, and mitigate the ethical, security, and operational risks associated with AI implementation.
- **Become a Change Agent:** Champion AI adoption in a way that empowers your people and positions your organization ahead of the competition.

Section 1: Demystifying AI for Strategic Advantage

You already know *why* AI is important. Now, let's focus on *how* it creates value. Generative AI is a subset of artificial intelligence that can create new, original content, from text and code to images and strategies, based on the patterns it learns from vast amounts of data.

Key Insight: Your role isn't to be the technical expert, but the **strategic translator** who connects AI's capabilities to your business objectives.

Real-World Power: Four Examples of Generative AI in the Workplace

1. **Hyper-Personalized Marketing:** Instead of generic email blasts, use GenAI to dynamically generate personalized product descriptions, ad copy, and entire campaign narratives tailored to specific customer segments.
2. **Accelerated R&D and Innovation:** In product development, use AI to brainstorm design concepts, simulate market responses to new features, or summarize complex research papers, drastically cutting down ideation time.
3. **Intelligent Business Intelligence:** Go beyond standard reports. Ask your AI tool in plain English, "What were the main reasons for customer churn in Q2, and what are three actionable strategies to improve retention?" and receive a synthesized analysis.
4. **Operational Efficiency through Automation:** Automate the drafting of routine reports, meeting summaries, and even code documentation, freeing your team to focus on high-value analysis and creative problem-solving.

Section 2: The Human Element: Leading Your Team Through the AI Transition

The single biggest barrier to AI adoption isn't technology, it's human fear.

Addressing the Three Core Fears:

- **Fear of Job Loss:** Be transparent. Reframe AI not as a replacement, but as a **powerful co-pilot**. Emphasize that AI will automate tasks, not roles. The focus will shift from *doing* the repetitive work to *managing, refining, and strategizing* based on AI-generated outputs.
    - **Your Action:** Host a workshop to identify repetitive tasks your team dislikes and brainstorm how AI could alleviate that burden.
- **Fear of Becoming Obsolete:** Acknowledge the learning curve. Commit to upskilling. Position AI proficiency as the most valuable new skill in the modern workforce and provide the resources and time to learn.

    - **Your Action:** Provide access to the free resources listed below and celebrate small learning milestones.
- **Fear of the "Black Box":** Be honest about the limitations. Discuss the potential for bias and errors ("hallucinations" in GenAI). This builds trust and positions you as a realistic, informed leader.

Inspiring Excitement: Share success stories from within your industry. When your team sees peers using AI to achieve remarkable results, it transforms from a threat into an opportunity for them to excel and stand out.

Section 3: A Manager's Framework for Responsible AI Implementation

Moving beyond ChatGPT means understanding the broader ecosystem and its risks.

A Simple Risk Mitigation Checklist:

- **Data Privacy & Security:** Never input sensitive, proprietary, or personal customer data into public, unsecured AI tools. Company data policies must be updated to reflect this.
- **Bias and Fairness:** Remember, AI models are trained on human-generated data, which can contain biases. Always have a human-in-the-loop to review AI-generated content for fairness and appropriateness, especially in HR or customer-facing applications.
- **Accuracy & "Hallucinations":** Generative AI can produce plausible-sounding but incorrect information. Establish a "trust but verify" protocol. Fact-check all critical outputs, especially numerical data, legal references, and technical specifications.
- **Intellectual Property:** Be aware of the ongoing legal debates around AI-generated content and copyright. Clarify ownership of AI-assisted work with your legal and leadership teams.

Your Action Plan & Toolkit

Expand Your Knowledge: Essential Resources for Managers

- **Harvard Business Review (AI & Machine Learning):** For high-level strategic articles on how AI is transforming business leadership. (**Website: `hbr.org`**)
- **MIT Sloan Management Review:** For research-driven insights on managing technological change and digital transformation. **(Website: `sloanreview.mit.edu`)**
- **The AI Pedagogy Project (by Harvard):** A fantastic collection of resources and critical perspectives to understand AI's capabilities and missteps**. (Website: `aipedagogy.org`)**

- **One Useful Thing (Ethan Mollick's Substack):** A highly accessible and insightful newsletter from a Wharton professor, focusing on the practical implications of Generative AI for work and education.

Conclusion: From Manager to AI-Empowered Leader

Your journey with AI is not a technical sprint but a leadership marathon. By mastering the fundamentals, addressing your team's human concerns with empathy, and implementing AI with a clear-eyed view of both its power and its pitfalls, you will do more than just adopt a new technology. You will future-proof your team, inspire innovation, and secure a decisive competitive advantage. The future belongs to leaders who can harness intelligence, both human and artificial.

The AI-Powered Expert

Your Ultimate Guide to Working Smarter, Not Harder

Forget the fear of robots taking your job. The future belongs to professionals who partner with AI, using it as a force multiplier for their skills, creativity, and strategic impact. This chapter isn't about adding more to your plate; it's about transforming how you work. By integrating AI as a collaborative **"coworker,"** you can reclaim your time, amplify your productivity, and future-proof your career.

Here's how you will transform your workday:

Reclaim Your Most Precious Resource: Time

Stop spending your valuable hours on repetitive, manual tasks. By automating processes like data entry, email filtering, meeting summarization, and report generation, you can **save over 10 hours each week**. Imagine what you could do with an extra 10 hours, focus on strategy, learn a new skill, or simply achieve a better work-life balance.

Amplify Your Productivity and Impact

AI allows you to streamline your entire workday. It handles the administrative grind, freeing you to concentrate on the high-impact, human-centric work that drives real value, building relationships, making complex decisions, and developing innovative strategies. Shift from being a **"doer"** to a **"strategist."**

Ignite Your Creative Spark

Hit a creative block? AI can be your brainstorming partner. Use it to generate fresh marketing angles, outline project proposals, suggest design variations, or overcome writer's block. It's not about replacing your ideas but enhancing them, providing a springboard for true innovation.

Future-Proof Your Career

Proficiency with AI is no longer a niche skill; it's a core competency for the modern workforce. By acquiring the ability to effectively leverage AI tools, you are not just keeping up, you are positioning yourself as a forward-thinking leader, making yourself indispensable in an AI-driven economy.

Master the Art of the Prompt

The key to unlocking AI's potential lies in how you communicate with it. We will demystify the process of crafting effective prompts. You'll develop techniques to move from vague requests to precise, contextual instructions that yield high-quality, usable outputs, turning you from a casual user into a power user.

Build Mastery with Minimal Time Investment

We know you're busy. That's why our method is built on **10 minutes a day of hands-on practice**. Through bite-sized, practical drills, you will build confidence and skill without overwhelming your schedule. Consistency trumps intensity, and in just a few weeks, using AI will become second nature.

Quantify Your Growth with Your "AIQ"

How do you know you're improving? You'll take an **AIQ (Artificial Intelligence Quotient) assessment** at the beginning and end of your journey. This tangible metric will allow you to measure your growth in understanding, application, and strategic use of AI, showcasing your enhanced capabilities.

Your New AI Coworkers: A Team of Six

Learn to delegate to a team of AI specialists that work for you 24/7:

The Administrative Assistant: Manages your calendar, drafts routine emails, and organizes your inbox.

Tools to Explore:

- **Grammarly**: Goes beyond grammar to refine tone and clarity in communications.
- **Claude**: Excellent for summarizing long documents and emails.
- **The Planner/Strategist:** Helps you map out projects, identify potential risks, and develop strategic outlines.

Tools to Explore:

- **ChatGPT** or **Microsoft Copilot**: Ideal for brainstorming, creating project plans, and generating SWOT analyses.
- **The Copy Editor:** Polishes your writing, ensures consistency of tone, and checks for grammatical errors and clarity.

Tools to Explore:

- **Hemingway Editor**: Helps you write more clearly and concisely.
- **ProWritingAid**: Offers in-depth style and grammar checking.
- **The Data Analyst:** Processes and visualizes data, identifies trends, and generates initial insights from spreadsheets and reports.

Tools to Explore:

- **Microsoft Excel's Analyze Data** (formerly Ideas): Uses AI to create instant charts and summaries.
- **Tableau**: Powerful for creating advanced, interactive data visualizations.
- **The Researcher:** Quickly synthesizes information on any topic, providing summaries and sourcing key facts.

Tools to Explore:

- **Perplexity AI**: Excellent for research with its focus on providing sources and citations.
- **Consensus**: Uses AI to find and summarize insights from peer-reviewed academic research.
- **The Tech Support Agent:** Explains error codes, troubleshoots common software issues, and generates simple code snippets.

Tools to Explore:

- **GitHub Copilot**: Acts as an AI pair programmer, suggesting code and functions.
- **Google Bard**: Integrated with Google's suite, useful for troubleshooting and explaining technical concepts.

Today, you won't just be reading about AI, you will be actively collaborating with it, equipped with the skills and resources to build a more efficient, creative, and impactful career.

Chapter 2

THE AI MARKETING REVOLUTION

Transforming Your Strategy and Skyrocketing Growth

Chapter Introduction

The marketing landscape is undergoing a massive shift, powered by Artificial Intelligence. No longer a futuristic concept, AI is a practical, powerful tool that is leveling the playing field and giving businesses of all sizes an unprecedented advantage. This chapter will guide you beyond the hype and into the practical application of AI. You will learn how to leverage these intelligent tools to automate tedious tasks, generate insightful data, create compelling content at scale, and ultimately, drive sustainable business growth by connecting with your audience in more meaningful and effective ways.

1. Hyper-Personalized Customer Engagement

AI excels at analyzing vast amounts of data to understand individual customer preferences and behaviors. This allows you to move beyond generic, one-size-fits-all marketing and into the realm of hyper-personalization.

- **Email Marketing Optimization:** AI tools can analyze each subscriber's past behavior to determine the **ideal time to deliver an email**, significantly boosting open rates. They can also personalize subject lines and content recommendations to resonate with each individual.
- **Understanding Customer Behavior:** By tracking user interactions on your website and social media, AI can identify patterns, predict future actions, and help you make data-driven decisions faster than ever before.

Helpful Resource: HubSpot offers robust marketing automation with AI-driven insights for personalization. https://www.hubspot.com/products/marketing

2. Content Creation at Warp Speed

Content is king, but creating it is time-consuming. AI-powered writing assistants are revolutionizing this process, allowing you to produce high-quality, relevant content 5x faster.

- **SEO-Friendly Blog Posts:** Generate outlines, full drafts, and meta descriptions optimized for search engines in minutes, not hours.

- **Engaging Social Media Content:** Automatically create dozens of post captions, ideas for images, and even video scripts tailored to your brand's voice for platforms like Instagram, Facebook, and LinkedIn.
- **Sales and Ad Copy:** From crafting compelling sales page text to generating multiple variants of Facebook and Google ad copy, AI can A/B test ideas at the conceptual stage to find the most persuasive messaging.

Helpful Resource: Jasper (formerly Jarvis) is a leading AI content platform designed specifically for marketers. https://www.jasper.ai

3. Dominating Search Engines and Outranking Competitors

Gaining visibility on Google is a constant battle. AI provides a strategic edge by giving you a clear roadmap to the top of the search results.

Competitor Content Analysis: Advanced AI tools can dissect the content of the pages currently outranking you. They **discover the exact changes you need to make**, such as covering missing topics, improving readability, or optimizing for better keywords, to climb the rankings and secure the #1 spot.

Helpful Resource: https://www.frase.io and **Surfer SEO** are excellent AI-driven tools for content optimization and SEO analysis. (https://www.frase.io | https://surferseo.com)

4. Automating and Enhancing Customer Service

Instant, 24/7 customer support is no longer a luxury—it's an expectation. AI-powered chatbots and messaging systems can handle this load efficiently, improving customer satisfaction while freeing up your team.

- **Automated Customer Service:** AI can **take care of all your customer service requests** via chat on your website or through social media messaging. It can answer FAQs, track orders, and resolve common issues instantly.
- **Qualifying Leads and Sales:** These chatbots can also engage visitors, qualify leads by asking strategic questions, and even book appointments, seamlessly blending customer service with sales.

Helpful Resource: Intercom and **ManyChat** offer powerful AI chatbot solutions for websites and social media. (https://www.intercom.com | https://www.intercom.com)

Putting It All Together: A Practical Guide to ChatGPT for Marketers

ChatGPT has emerged as a versatile and accessible AI tool. Here's how you can leverage it to build a complete marketing campaign from beginning to end:

1. **Audience Investigation & Evaluation:** Prompt: "*Create a detailed buyer persona for a [Your Product/Service] targeting [Demographic]. Include their pain points, goals, and where they spend time online.*"
2. **Craft Optimized Social Media Content:** Prompt: "*Write 5 engaging Instagram captions for a new [Product] launch, using emojis and targeting [Your Audience].*"
3. **Generate an SEO-Friendly Blog Post:** Prompt: *"Write a 1,000-word blog post outline on the topic '[Your Topic]'. Include H2 and H3 headings and suggest primary and secondary keywords."*
4. **Create an Email Sequence:** Prompt: *"Draft a 3-part welcome email sequence for a new subscriber who downloaded our guide on [Topic]. The goal is to build trust and introduce our core service."*
5. **Design Sales Page Text:** Prompt: "*Write compelling headline and bullet-point benefits for a sales page for [Your Product], focusing on the transformation it provides.*"
6. **Develop Facebook & Google Ad Copy:** Prompt: "*Write 3 different versions of a short, punchy Google Ads headline and description for [Your Product] focusing on [Key Benefit].*"
7. **Examine Feedback & Enhance Offerings:** Prompt: "*Analyze the following customer reviews [Paste Reviews] and summarize the main strengths and weaknesses mentioned.*"

Important Note: While ChatGPT is a phenomenal starting point, always refine and infuse its output with your unique brand voice and real-world expertise. It is a collaborative tool, not a replacement for human judgment.

Conclusion: Your AI-Powered Future Starts Now

Integrating AI into your marketing strategy is not about replacing your creativity; it's about augmenting it. By embracing the tools and strategies outlined in this chapter, you can work smarter, not just harder. You will save countless hours, uncover hidden opportunities, and create more impactful marketing that resonates with your audience and drives tangible business results. The AI marketing revolution is here, it's time to join it.

Chapter 3

THE AI-POWERED FREELANCER

Building a Profitable Business with ChatGPT & Midjourney

Introduction

The freelance and online business landscape is undergoing a giant shift. Clients are no longer just looking for a service; they are looking for efficiency, scalability, and innovation. By integrating Artificial Intelligence, specifically language models like ChatGPT and image generators like Midjourney, you can position yourself as a cutting-edge professional. This chapter isn't about replacing your skills; it's about supercharging them. We will explore how to transform these AI tools from novelties into revenue-generating powerhouses, allowing you to offer more services, deliver higher quality work, and scale your business like never before.

Crafting Your AI Service Portfolio: From Ideas to Income

Here's a detailed breakdown of profitable freelance services you can build or enhance with ChatGPT, along with strategic insights and key resources.

1. The Copywriting Creator

Go beyond basic writing. Use ChatGPT to generate data-driven, persuasive copy that converts.

- **How to Use It:** Start with a detailed prompt. Instead of **"Write a product description,"** try: **"Write a 150-word product description for a [Product Name] targeting [Target Audience]. Highlight its eco-friendly materials, durability, and 30-day guarantee. Use a persuasive, enthusiastic tone and include a call-to-action to 'Shop Now.'"**
- **Service Offerings:** Website landing pages, sales letters, About Us pages, and product descriptions.
- **Pro Tip:** Use ChatGPT to A/B test different headlines and email subject lines before you even send them to a client.
- **Resource:** **https://www.copy.ai** and **https://www.jasper.ai** are dedicated AI copywriting platforms, but studying their output can help you refine your own ChatGPT prompts.

2. Social Media & Content Engine

Become a one-person content marketing agency. Keep your clients' social channels buzzing with fresh, engaging content.

How to Use It:

- **Content Calendars:** "Generate a 7-day Instagram content calendar for a vegan meal prep service. Include post ideas for Reels, Carousels, and Stories."
- **Post Captions & Hashtags:** "Write 5 engaging Instagram captions for a new coffee shop launch, including a mix of relevant and trending hashtags."
- **Service Offerings:** Monthly content calendars, individual post creation, video script ideas, and strategy documents.
- **Resource:** https://later.com **Blog** or **Hootsuite Blog** for understanding social media trends and best practices to inform your AI prompts.

3. Email Marketing Automation Specialist

Design and populate entire email sequences that nurture leads and drive sales.

How to Use It:

- **Welcome Series:** "Write a 3-email welcome sequence for a new SaaS product. Email 1: Thank you. Email 2: Explain the top 3 features. Email 3: Offer a live demo."
- **Newsletters & Promotions:** "Draft a weekly newsletter for a fitness coach announcing a new group challenge and including a healthy recipe."
- **Service Offerings:** Lead magnet nurturing sequences, promotional campaigns, weekly/bi-weekly newsletters, and cart abandonment emails.
- **Resource: ActiveCampaign** and **ConvertKit** have excellent blogs on email marketing strategy. Use their frameworks to structure your ChatGPT prompts.

4. Digital Product & Course Architect

Help experts package their knowledge into sellable digital products.

How to Use It: Use ChatGPT to outline, structure, and even draft modules for online courses, e-books, and workshops.

- **Prompt Example:** "Outline a 6-module online course for 'Beginner Digital Photography.' List the key lessons for each module."
- **Expand Content:** "Expand on Module 3, Lesson 2: 'Understanding Aperture,' by writing a 500-word explanation with practical examples."
- **Service Offerings:** Course curriculum design, e-book writing, worksheet and workbook creation.

- **Resource: Teachable** and **Thinkific** blogs offer great insights on what makes a successful online course structure.

5. Video Script & Ad Copy Virtuoso

The demand for video content is exploding. Provide the scripts that make videos engaging and ads effective.

How to Use It:

- **YouTube Videos:** "Write a script for a 5-minute YouTube video titled '5 Budgeting Mistakes Everyone Makes.' Structure it with a hook, the 5 points with explanations, and a conclusion."
- **Ad Copy (Note: Corrected from "Ads Copyright"):** "Write three 30-second video ad scripts for a new productivity app, each targeting a different pain point: time management, task organization, and team collaboration."
- **Service Offerings:** YouTube video scripts, TikTok/Reel scripts, paid social media ad copy.
- **Resource: Descript** is a powerful video editing tool that uses AI for editing and even generating voiceovers from text, a perfect companion to your scriptwriting service.

6. Sales Funnel Strategist

Map out the entire customer journey, from first click to final purchase.

How to Use It: ChatGPT can help you design the flow and write the copy for each stage of a funnel.

- **Prompt:** "Map out a sales funnel for a high-ticket coaching program. Describe the target audience, the lead magnet, the email nurture sequence, the sales page structure, and the follow-up sequence."
- **Service Offerings:** Sales funnel strategy documents, landing page copy for each funnel stage, and email sequence integration.
- **Resource: ClickFunnels** is the industry leader, and their blog and training materials are a masterclass in funnel building.

7. Web Presence Developer (Selling Pro Websites)

Combine ChatGPT with no-code website builders and Midjourney to offer complete web design packages.

How to Use It:

- **ChatGPT:** Generates all website content, Homepage, About, Services, FAQ, and Blog post.

- **Midjourney:** Creates unique, custom brand imagery, logos, and mockups based on prompts. (e.g., "/imagine a minimalist logo for a yoga studio named 'Serene Space', using soft greens and whites").
- **Service Offerings:** "Done-For-You" website packages on platforms like Wix, Shopify, or Webflow, including copy, basic SEO, and custom AI-generated imagery.
- **Resource: Webflow University** and **Wix Arena** are great for learning the technical side, while **Midjourney's Documentation** is essential for mastering AI image generation.

Key Websites for the AI Freelancer

- **For Learning Prompt Engineering:** https://learnprompting.org - A free, open-source course on communicating effectively with AI.
- **For AI News & Tools: Futurepedia** - A massive directory of the latest AI tools, updated daily.
- **For Freelance Business Growth: Upwork** and **Fiverr** - Use these platforms not just for jobs, but to research what AI-related services are in high demand.
- **For Community & Inspiration: Reddit Communities** like r/ChatGPT, r/Midjourney, and r/freelance are invaluable for seeing what others are creating and solving common problems.

The AI Cashflow Engine Monetizing Midjourney for Freelancers and Entrepreneurs

The dream of the digital creator is to transform imagination into income, swiftly and scalably. Midjourney AI isn't just a tool for generating stunning art; it's a powerful engine for your freelance or online business. This section moves beyond theory and into actionable strategies, showing you how to leverage this AI to build multiple streams of revenue, from passive side-hustles to core business services.

From Prompt to Profit: Your First Steps

Before the revenue flows, you must master the machine. Your journey begins not with a sale, but with a **`/imagine`** command. Dedicate time to learning prompt engineering, the art of crafting detailed, descriptive text that guides the AI to your desired output. Understand parameters like **`--ar`** for aspect ratio (crucial for social media posts vs. print-on-demand products) and **`--style`** to fine-tune the aesthetic. This foundational skill is what separates amateur images from sellable assets.

Revenue Stream 1: The Digital Product & Print-on-Demand Empire

This is the most accessible starting point for many, creating products with virtually no overhead.

- **Selling Your Art:** Generate unique, high-quality artwork and sell it as digital downloads (wallpapers, social media packs, Procreate brushes) on platforms like Etsy or Gumroad. The key is to find a niche, think **"Cottagecore landscapes," "cyberpunk character portraits,"** or "art deco patterns."
- **Best-Selling T-Shirts & Merchandise:** Move beyond generic designs. Use Midjourney to create hyper-specific themes that resonate with dedicated communities (e.g., **"D&D Warlock Cat Lover," "Vintage Sailing Ship Diagram").** Upload your designs to **Print-on-Demand (POD)** services that handle printing, shipping, and customer service, leaving you to focus on marketing.
- **Helpful Websites: Redbubble**, **Teepublic**, **Printful**, and **Merch by Amazon** are leading POD platforms. Use **Trello** or **Google Sheets** to organize your designs and track best-sellers.

Revenue Stream 2: Supercharging Your Freelance Services

Integrate Midjourney into your existing freelance workflow to deliver more value, faster, and attract higher-paying clients.

- **Revolutionizing Graphic Design:** Don't just design; conceptualize. Use Midjourney to generate unique logo concepts, brand mood boards, custom icons, and stunning poster designs. Present clients with multiple AI-generated concepts in seconds, drastically reducing initial brainstorming time and positioning yourself as a cutting-edge creator.
- **Creating Ideal Customer Profiles (ICPs) & Marketing Assets:** Go beyond stock photos. For marketers and agencies, use Midjourney to generate photorealistic images of a client's "ideal customer" in specific scenarios. Imagine creating a perfect image of "a sustainable fashion blogger in a minimalist apartment" or "a tech CEO hiking a mountain." This makes target audience presentations incredibly tangible and impactful.

Revenue Stream 3: Building Digital Assets & Audiences

This stream focuses on creating long-term, valuable online properties.

Build and Monetize an AI Influencer: This is an advanced but highly lucrative strategy. Use Midjourney to create a consistent and compelling character. Develop a unique name, backstory, and aesthetic for this persona.

1. **Creation:** Generate hundreds of images of your AI influencer in different outfits, locations, and scenarios to build a content library.
2. **Content:** Use a second **AI Tool** like ChatGPT to write captions and posts in your influencer's **"voice."**
3. **Platforms:** Post consistently on visual platforms like Instagram, Pinterest, or TikTok.

4. **Monetization:** Once an audience is built, monetize through sponsored posts, affiliate marketing, selling the digital assets (the images themselves as stock photos), or even **"merch"** featuring the influencer's face.
5. **Helpful Websites:** Use **Canva** for easy social media post design, **Buffer** or **Hootsuite** for scheduling, and leverage **social media analytics** tools (like Instagram Insights or Twitter Analytics) to understand what content resonates and refine your strategy.

Your Essential Toolkit for Success

To execute these strategies effectively, pair Midjourney with other powerful, often free, tools:

- **For Image Upscaling & Enhancement:** https://www.upscale.media or **Let's Enhance** can increase the resolution of your Midjourney creations for high-quality prints.
- **For Graphic Design & Touch-Ups: Canva** (for easy design) and **GIMP** (a free, powerful alternative to Photoshop) are essential for adding text, removing small flaws, or combining AI elements.
- **For Niche & Keyword Research:** Use **Everbee** (for Etsy) or **Helium 10** (for Amazon) to discover what people are actually searching for, ensuring your AI creations have a ready market.

- The power of Midjourney lies in its ability to decouple creation time from value. By combining your unique creative vision with these strategic frameworks, you can skyrocket your business, turning the AI's endless generation into your enduring revenue.

Conclusion: You are the Conductor

ChatGPT and Midjourney are your orchestra, capable of playing any tune you direct. Your value as a freelancer is no longer just in execution, but in your **strategy, curation, and human touch**. You refine the AI's output, ensure it aligns with the client's brand voice, and infuse it with creativity and emotional intelligence that AI lacks. By mastering these tools, you are not being replaced; you are evolving into a more powerful, efficient, and invaluable business partner. Now go and build the future of your freelance business.

Chapter 4

The Automated Empire

Building AI-Powered Passive Income Streams in 2025

Chapter Introduction

The dream of earning money while you sleep is no longer a fantasy reserved for a lucky few. The advent of Artificial Intelligence has democratized the tools for creation, automation, and scale, allowing savvy entrepreneurs to build diversified income portfolios with unprecedented efficiency. This chapter is your blueprint. We will move beyond theory and into actionable strategies, exploring multiple business models where AI acts as your co-founder, creative director, and automated workforce. Prepare to master the concept of modern online wealth: digital products, content empires, and automated service delivery.

The Digital Product Engine: Create Once, Sell Forever

The cornerstone of passive income is the digital product. AI supercharges your ability to create high-quality, in-demand products at a fraction of the time and cost.

The AI-Powered Print-on-Demand Store

Leverage image generators like **Midjourney** and **Leonardo AI** to create stunning, niche-specific designs for t-shirts, mugs, and posters. Platforms like **Redbubble** and **Amazon Merch on Demand** handle printing and shipping, meaning you never touch inventory.

- **AI Tools:** Midjourney, Leonardo AI, Stable Diffusion, DALL-E 3.
- **Key Strategy:** Use ChatGPT to brainstorm hyper-specific niches (e.g., "minimalist cat lover astronomy designs") and generate dozens of design concepts in a single session.

The AI Author: E-books & Low-Content Books

Dominate Amazon KDP by using ChatGPT to outline, draft, and even write entire non-fiction books or story frameworks. For journals, planners, and coloring books (low-content), use AI to generate intricate patterns and interior layouts.

- **AI Tools:** ChatGPT (Claude 2 is excellent for long-form writing), Jasper, Sudowrite.
- **Key Strategy:** Combine AI writing with a human touch for editing, voice, and fact-checking to create a superior product.

The Audiobook Narrator & Music Composer

Transform your AI-written e-books into audiobooks using ultra-realistic voice synthesis from **Eleven Labs**. Alternatively, compose royalty-free background music for YouTube videos and sell it on platforms like **AudioJungle** using tools like **Soundraw** or **AIVA**.

- **AI Tools:** Eleven Labs, Murf AI, Soundraw, AIVA.
- **Helpful Websites: ACX** (for audiobook distribution), **AudioJungle** (to sell music and sound effects).

The Online Course Creator

Use AI to drastically reduce course creation time. ChatGPT can help you structure curriculum, write scripts, and create quizzes. **Canva's AI Magic Write** and presentation tools can design your slides, while AI video tools can help with editing.

- **AI Tools:** ChatGPT, Canva Magic Write, CapCut's AI editing features.
- **Helpful Websites: Teachable**, **Thinkific**, **Udemy** (platforms to host and sell your courses).

The Content & Traffic Flywheel

Automate Your Audience Growth

Content is the fuel for the digital economy. AI allows you to produce it consistently, optimize it for discovery, and monetize the audience you build.

The Automated YouTube Channel

From ideation to publication, AI can handle every step. Use ChatGPT for video script ideas, **Leonardo AI** for custom thumbnails, **Eleven Labs** for voiceovers, and **CapCut** or **Descript** for AI-powered video editing and transcription.

- **AI Tools:** TubeBuddy (for SEO), VidIQ, Pictory (for turning text/blog posts into videos).
- **Key Strategy:** Focus on evergreen, search-based niches (e.g., "how-to" guides, explanations) where AI-generated visuals and voiceovers are highly effective.

The AI-Optimized Blog

Generate article ideas, outlines, and full drafts with ChatGPT. Use SEO plugins like **AIOSEO** or tools like **Frase.io** and **Surfer SEO** to research keywords and optimize your content to rank #1 on Google.

- **AI Tools:** ChatGPT, Claude 2, Frase.io, Surfer SEO.
- **Monetization:** Display ads (Google AdSense), affiliate marketing, or promoting your own digital products.

Pinterest Automation for Viral Traffic

Pinterest is a visual search engine. Use AI tools like **Tailwind** to generate dozens of fresh pin designs from a single blog post or product link and schedule them for automatic posting to drive consistent, passive traffic.

- **AI Tools:** Canva (for batch-creating designs), Tailwind's AI SmartSchedule.
- **Helpful Websites: Pinterest for Business** (their official analytics and best practices hub).

The Automated Service Model: Scale Your Freelance Skills

Turn your freelance gig into a scalable agency by automating the delivery and leveraging AI to handle repetitive tasks.

The AI-Augmented Freelancer (Writing, Video, Design)

Whether you're a writer, video editor, or graphic designer, use AI to 10x your output. Writers use ChatGPT for research and first drafts; video editors use **CapCut** and **Descript** for auto-captioning and scene editing; designers use **Canva** and **Adobe Firefly** to rapidly prototype ideas.

- **AI Tools:** As above, plus GrammarlyGO for editing, Adobe Podcast for audio enhancement.

The AI Social Media Marketing Agency (SMMA)

Offer client services like content creation, ad copywriting, and performance analysis. Use AI to generate a month's worth of social media posts, write dozens of ad variations, and create performance reports in minutes.

- **AI Tools:** ChatGPT (for copy), AdCreative.ai (for generating ad creatives), Metricool (for scheduling and analytics).

The AI Funnel Creator

Build high-converting sales funnels for digital products and online courses. Use AI copywriters to craft compelling email sequences, landing page copy, and ad copy that guides the customer seamlessly from awareness to purchase.

- **AI Tools:** Jasper (excellent for marketing copy), Copy.ai, Systeme.io (all-in-one funnel builder with AI features).
- **Helpful Websites: ClickFunnels**, **Kartra** (other powerful funnel-building platforms).

Advanced AI Monetization

The Affiliate & Advertising Edge

For those comfortable with digital marketing fundamentals, these models offer high-reward potential.

AI-Driven CPA (Cost Per Action) Marketing

Use AI to analyze which affiliate offers are converting best. AI tools can help you create massive amounts of targeted landing page content and ad copy to test and scale winning campaigns on platforms like Taboola or Outbrain.

- **Helpful Websites: MaxBounty**, **ClickBank** (popular CPA networks).

Hyper-Targeted Social Media Advertising

Platforms like Meta Ads Manager and Google Ads have powerful AI built-in for audience targeting and bidding. Your role shifts to feeding the AI with high-quality creative assets (which you can generate with tools like **AdCreative.ai** and analyzing the data to guide its learning.

Your AI Toolbox for 2025 Mastery

- **Ideation & Content Creation: ChatGPT**, **Claude 2**
- **Visuals & Design: Midjourney**, **Leonardo AI**, **Canva**, **DALL-E 3**
- **Audio & Voice: Eleven Labs**, **Murf AI**
- **Video Production: CapCut**, **Descript**, **Pictory**
- **Marketing & SEO: Jasper**, **Frase.io**, **Surfer SEO**, **AdCreative.ai**

Conclusion

The models outlined here are not mutually exclusive; the most powerful automated empires are built by combining them. An AI-generated ebook can be turned into an audiobook, promoted by an AI-run YouTube channel, and sold through an AI-optimized blog. In 2025, your most valuable asset is not just your effort, but your strategic command over the AI tools that multiply it. Start with one model, master the workflow, and then scale into your own automated empire.

Section 2

The Blueprint For Financial Success

Chapter 5

The Missing Education

The 7 Financial Skills for a Wealthy Life

Introduction: The Financial Lessons We Never Got

Think back to your high school years. You were likely required to dissect a frog, memorize the periodic table, and analyze Shakespearean plays. While these subjects have their place, they often overshadowed the most critical lesson of all: how to build a successful financial life.

The U.S. public school system was the institution best positioned to equip us with the tools for financial independence, from personal budgeting and investing to the fundamentals of starting a business. These are the skills we use every day, yet they were evidently absent from the standard curriculum. Instead of **"Business 101,"** the focus shifted to standardized testing and common core subjects, leaving generations of Americans to figure out money on their own, often through costly trial and error.

The consequences of this gap in our education are staggering:

- Did you know that **67% of American families** do not have $1,000 in savings to cover an emergency?
- A vast majority of the population is shackled by massive monthly payments toward mortgages, student debt, credit cards, and auto loans, making the dream of financial independence feel distant.

This chapter is about reclaiming that missing education. We will explore the seven foundational financial skills that should have been a core part of your high school experience. Mastering these is the first step toward breaking the cycle of living paycheck-to-paycheck and building lasting personal wealth.

The 7 Essential Financial Skills

1. Taming the Plastic: Understanding Credit Cards & Interest

Credit cards are not free money; they are high-interest loans in disguise. As of 2023, Americans owe over **$1 trillion in credit card debt**. The average household carrying a balance owes significantly more than $7,000.

The Problem: The minimum payment is a trap. When you only pay the minimum, you're mostly covering the interest, not the principal. A $5,000 debt at 18% APR could take over 20 years to pay off if you only make minimum payments, costing you thousands in extra interest.

The Skill: Use credit cards for convenience and rewards, **never** for debt you can't pay off immediately. Always strive to pay your balance in full each month. Understand your card's Annual Percentage Rate (APR) and how compound interest works *against* you as a borrower.

- **Helpful Resource:** Use a **credit card payoff calculator** from sites like https://www.nerdwallet.com or https://www.bankrate.com to see how long it will take to pay off your debt and how much interest you'll pay.

2. Your Financial GPA: Building a Stellar Credit Score

Your FICO score (ranging from 300 to 850) is your financial report card. Lenders, landlords, and even some employers use it to judge your reliability.

- **300-579 (Poor):** You will have difficulty getting approved for loans and will pay the highest interest rates.
- **580-669 (Fair):** You may qualify, but not for the best terms.
- **670-739 (Good):** You'll qualify for most loans with decent rates.
- **740-799 (Very Good):** You'll receive favorable rates and terms.
- **800-850 (Exceptional):** The financial red carpet is rolled out for you.

The Skill: Build your score by paying all bills on time, keeping your credit card balances low (ideally below 30% of your limit), and only applying for new credit when necessary.

- **Helpful Resource:** You can get a free credit report annually from https://www.annualcreditreport.com/index.action . Services like https://www.creditkarma.com or your credit card issuer often provide free weekly score updates and monitoring.

3. Telling Your Money Where to Go: The Art of Budgeting

A budget isn't a restriction; it's a plan for your freedom. It's the simple act of understanding your **income** and directing your **expenses**.

The Skill: Adopt a budgeting method that works for you.

- **50/30/20 Rule:** 50% of income for needs, 30% for wants, and 20% for savings/debt repayment.
- **Zero-Based Budget:** Every dollar of income is assigned a job (savings, bills, fun) so your income minus your expenses equals zero.
- **Helpful Resource:** Apps like https://mint.intuit.com or https://www.ynab.com automate tracking and help you stick to your plan.

4. Financial Awareness: The Modern "Checkbook Balancing"

While we write fewer paper checks today, the principle is more important than ever. **"Balancing your checkbook"** now means having real-time awareness of your cash flow.

The Skill: Regularly review your bank and credit card statements. Track every transaction, both incoming and outgoing. Set up low-balance alerts with your bank to avoid overdraft fees, which are a massive drain on your finances.

- **Helpful Resource:** Your bank's mobile app is your best tool. Use it to monitor transactions daily. For a more holistic view, the budgeting apps listed above are also excellent for this.

5. The World's Most Powerful Force: Compound Interest

Albert Einstein reportedly called compound interest the **"Eighth wonder of the world**." It's when your interest starts earning its own interest, creating a snowball effect on your wealth.

The Skill: Understand the **Rule of 72**. Divide 72 by your annual rate of return to find how many years it will take for your money to double.

- *Example:* At a 7% return, 72 ÷ 7 ≈ 10.2 years. An investment of $10,000 would grow to $20,000 in about 10 years, without you adding another dollar.
- The key is to start early. Time is the most critical ingredient in the compound interest recipe.
- **Helpful Resource:** Play with a **compound interest calculator** from https://www.investor.gov to see the dramatic impact of starting early versus waiting.

6. Making Your Money Work for You: The Basics of Investing

The wealthy don't just save money; they put it to work. The primary vehicles for this are paper assets like stocks, bonds, and low-cost index funds or ETFs (Exchange-Traded Funds).

The Skill: Shift your mindset from **"I can't afford to invest"** to **"I can't afford *not* to invest."** Learn the basics of asset classes and the power of diversification (not putting all your eggs in one basket). The goal is not to become a day trader but a consistent, long-term investor.

- **Helpful Resource:** For beginners, https://www.bogleheads.org/blog/portfolio/the-bogleheads-guide-to-investing is an invaluable, no-nonsense resource. Apps like https://www.acorns.com or https://www.stash.com can help you start investing with small amounts of money.

7. Becoming the Boss: The Fundamentals of Starting a Business

The entire economy runs on businesses, yet we were never taught how to start one. Understanding basic concepts like business planning, budgeting for a startup, and customer acquisition could have empowered millions to create their own jobs.

The Skill: Recognize that a business solves a problem or fills a need. Learn the basics of creating a simple business plan, separating personal and business finances, and the principles of marketing.

- **Helpful Resource:** The U.S. **https://www.sba.gov/business-guide/plan-your-business** offers free guides and tools on every step of starting a business. **https://www.score.org** provides free mentorship from experienced business professionals.

Conclusion: Your Education Starts Now

Our traditional education system failed us by neglecting these vital life skills. But your financial education doesn't have to end here. The most powerful step you can take is to accept responsibility for your own financial IQ.

The knowledge is out there, waiting for you to claim it. By mastering these seven skills, you move from being a passenger in your financial life to the driver. You can break the cycle of debt, build wealth, and create a future of financial security and independence.

Ready to take control? We have compiled a detailed **"Empowerment Resource List"** at the end of this book, featuring our top-recommended books, websites, and tools for mastering your money and potentially starting your own business. Your journey to financial literacy begins today.

Chapter 6

The Hidden Curriculum

What Our School System Didn't Teach Us

About Life, Money, and Power

Introduction: The Mandate of Compulsory Education

In the United States, the path of a young person is largely predefined by law. Compulsory education statutes require attendance at a public or private school from approximately ages 5 to 16, with the threat of legal consequences for parents who do not comply. The school system we have all participated into, was born from noble intentions to create an educated citizenry, places immense trust in our teachers to guide and equip the next generation.

We depend on these educators to provide the knowledge and skills necessary for a successful and intelligent life. The unspoken promise is that a diploma signifies readiness, readiness to secure a job in a fulfilling field, earn a sustainable living, and someday support a family. But is this promise fully delivered?

The Architect of the Classroom: Who Sets the Agenda?

It's a common misconception that your local teacher designs the curriculum. In reality, your school teachers and principals are employees within a vast, decentralized system. While the **U.S. Department of Education** sets broad national policy and provides funding, curricular mandates are primarily determined at the **state and local level** by entities like State Boards of Education and local school districts.

This means that every public school teacher is required to follow a mandated curriculum, a **"hidden script"** handed down from authorities. This script prioritizes standardized test scores in core subjects like math, science, and language arts, often at the expense of practical, life-altering skills. The teacher, however intelligent and well-intentioned, is an employee of this system, not an independent entrepreneur free to teach what they please.

The Missing Pages in Our Education: Critical Skills for a Successful Life

The central flaw in this system is not what it includes, but what it omits. We spent years learning algebra and the dates of historical battles, but were left unarmed for the actual battles of adult life. The curriculum we followed was designed to create well-rounded students, but not necessarily self-sufficient adults.

Here are the critical subjects that were largely absent from our compulsory education:

1. The Entrepreneurial Mindset vs. The Employee Mentality

The system's implicit goal is to prepare you for a job, not to create jobs. Businesses provide nearly all the products and services we need, yet the mechanics of business ownership, creating an idea, securing financing, understanding operations, and managing cash flow, are treated as niche topics for college business schools, not essential life skills.

This creates a population of job-seekers instead of job-creators. Understanding business could have been a game-changer, providing an alternative path for those with the drive to build something of their own, with the **"job option"** remaining a valid choice, not the only one.

- **Resource to Explore:** The **Kauffman Foundation** is a leading organization focused on education and entrepreneurship. Their website offers a wealth of research and resources on fostering an entrepreneurial mindset. **https://www.kauffman.org**

2. Financial Literacy: The Language of Life

We are all acutely aware that modern life requires money. From housing and food to transportation, family, and even death, every facet of existence has a cost. Yet, we were never formally taught the language of money.

Why weren't **"Financial Operations 101**" and **"Personal Investing"** required courses? We needed to learn:

- How to create and manage a personal budget.
- The power of compound interest and long-term investing.
- The difference between an asset and a liability.
- How taxes and credit scores work.
- Basic retirement planning.

This knowledge is not just about getting rich; it's about achieving stability and freedom from perpetual financial anxiety.

- **Resource to Explore: https://www.mymoney.gov** is the U.S. government's website dedicated to teaching all Americans the basics about financial education. It's a fantastic, non-commercial starting point.

3. Practical Life and Communication Skills

Life skills consist of the practical knowledge needed to navigate the world independently. For many children from stable homes, these are taught by parents. But for those from broken or disadvantaged homes, school may be their only hope to learn them.

These essential skills include:

- Effective communication and conflict resolution.
- Critical thinking and informed decision-making.
- Basic cooking, nutrition, and household maintenance.
- Automobile maintenance (e.g., changing a tire, checking oil).
- Basic sewing and mending.

These are not "**soft skills";** they are survival skills that build confidence and self-reliance.

4. Interpersonal Relationships and Emotional Intelligence

The statistic is sobering: nearly 50% of marriages in the U.S. end in divorce, often citing money issues, infidelity, and abuse as primary causes. What if we had been taught the architecture of a healthy relationship in school?

Education in emotional intelligence, how to manage emotions, practice empathy, communicate needs, and resolve conflicts respectfully, could have transformative effects. It teaches how to deal with a bully, understand someone from a different background, and build compassion instead of responding with anger and bitterness.

- **Resource to Explore:** The **Collaborative for Academic, Social, and Emotional Learning (CASEL)** is a trusted source for research and tools on integrating social-emotional learning into education. https://casel.org

A Tale of Two Systems: The Education of the Wealthy

It is instructive to look at the education received by many children from wealthy families. Often attending elite private schools, their curriculum frequently emphasizes critical thinking, leadership, and financial wisdom. They are taught to be owners, bankers, and investors, to make their money work for them.

The wealthy often remain wealthy because they are taught, from a young age, the principles of asset building and investment. This contrasts sharply with the public school focus on preparing students to be competent employees who trade their time for a paycheck.

Conclusion: Taking Ownership of Your Own Education

The reality is that the public-school system is designed with a specific outcome in mind: to create a literate, employable workforce. It was not designed to create financially independent entrepreneurs or emotionally intelligent life masters.

Remember, your teachers were dedicated but bound by the mandates of the system they served. They could only teach you the script they were given. The responsibility for your education does not end with a diploma. You must now become the teacher and the student of your own life.

Take ownership. Actively seek out the knowledge of business, finance, and personal development that was absent from your formal schooling. Do not wait for this valuable information to be handed to you; the system is not built to provide it. Your future success and freedom depend on your willingness to write the final chapters of your education yourself.

Chapter 7

The Unspoken Rules of Money

Shifting from a Consumer to an Owner Mindset

Introduction: The Daily Money Grind

Most of us work tirelessly in our jobs and businesses, striving to earn more money, build wealth, and secure our financial futures. But what is money, truly? For the vast majority, it's simply a medium of exchange, a tool to acquire the goods and services we need to live. Approximately 90% of working-class Americans, and millions more around the globe, wake up each day to trade their time, energy, and skills for a paycheck. This routine, working for someone else to ensure our survival, is the default setting for our society.

The pursuit of money is the engine of our world. It fuels our economies and dictates the rhythm of our lives. This drive compels us to purchase the essentials for survival: shelter, food, clothing, transportation, and even entertainment. Yet, while everyone is running this race, only a few seem to know the secret paths that lead to lasting prosperity.

The Great Divide: Why the Wealthy Stay Wealthy

The gap between the rich and the working poor isn't just about the amount of money they have; it's about their fundamental understanding of how money operates. Wealthy individuals remain wealthy because they focus on creating and acquiring **assets**, things that put money *into* their pockets. They spend their time developing systems, businesses, and investments that generate multiple streams of revenue.

Conversely, the working poor often remain in their condition not due to a lack of effort, but due to a gap in financial education. Without the proper training on how money works, they remain trapped in a cycle of trading time for money. Their primary focus is on their **job**, not on building assets that work for them. The key is to shift from being a passive earner to an active builder, to spend time brainstorming ideas, developing valuable skill-sets, and bringing something new to the marketplace.

The Golden Rule: Make Money Work For You

The wealthy understand a critical rule that eludes many: **Money flows to those who understand it and know how to make it work for them, rather than them working for it.**

The secret involves a two-step mental shift:

1. **Defensive Finance:** Learn how to keep more of the money you already earn. This means mastering budgeting, minimizing taxes legally, and avoiding debt traps.
2. **Offensive Finance:** Learn how to maximize and grow your money by acquiring income-generating assets. This is where the magic of **compound interest** comes into play, often called the eighth wonder of the world, as it allows your earnings to generate their own earnings over time.

The Shield of the Wealthy: Protecting Your Assets

Wealthy individuals spend little time worrying about rising costs or bills not because they ignore them, but because they are insulated by their assets. A crucial, often overlooked, strategy they use is legal protection for their wealth. One of the most effective tools is a **living trust**.

A living trust is not just for the ultra-rich; it's a key part of a sound financial plan. Set up with a legal professional, it allows you to:

- **Maintain Privacy:** Avoid the public, court-supervised process of probate.
- **Protect from Lawsuits:** Shield your assets from potential creditors and legal judgments.
- **Ensure Smooth Transition:** Dictate exactly how your assets are managed and distributed, both during your life and after.

The Root of the Problem: A Missing Education

Reflect on your school years. How much time was dedicated to learning about savings accounts, investment vehicles, asset classes, or credit management? For most of us, the answer is little to none. Our education focused on arithmetic, science, and literature, preparing us to be employees, not financial experts.

This systemic lack of financial literacy is the primary reason so many struggle with money management today. We were taught how to be good consumers and reliable employees, but not how to be investors and business owners.

Understanding the System You're In

It's crucial to recognize that we live within a framework designed by governments, financial institutions, and large corporations. The rules of this game, from tax laws to investment vehicles, were often shaped by powerful interests long before we arrived. Without an awareness of these systems, we are merely players on a field whose boundaries we don't understand. The goal is not to succumb to doubt, but to educate oneself about these rules to use them to your advantage.

The Inescapable Reality: Money is Required for Everything

From the food you eat to the roof over your head, and even the cost of your own burial, every facet of modern life requires money. This isn't meant to be depressing, but to highlight a fundamental truth: mastering money is not a hobby; it is a core survival skill in the 21st century. Since your life and choices are so deeply intertwined with finance, making its study a priority is one of the most empowering decisions you can make.

Becoming Fluent: Learning the Language of Money

To command money, you must first understand its language. You don't need to become a Wall Street expert overnight, but you must grasp key concepts. Here are some essential terms to add to your vocabulary:

- **Asset vs. Liability:** An asset puts money *in* your pocket (e.g., a rental property). A liability takes money *out* of your pocket (e.g., your car loan).
- **Compound Interest:** The process where you earn interest on your initial investment *and* on the interest that investment has already earned.
- **Return on Investment (ROI):** A measure of the profitability of an investment.
- **Liquidity:** How quickly an asset can be converted to cash.

Your Toolkit: Resources to Build Your Financial IQ

To Learn the Fundamentals:

- **Investopedia:** The definitive online resource for financial terms and concepts.
- **Khan Academy:** Offers free courses on finance and economics.
- **https://www.mymoney.gov :** The U.S. government's website dedicated to financial education.

To Start and Grow a Business:

- https://www.score.org : Provides free mentorship from retired business executives.
- **U.S. Small Business Administration (https://www.sba.gov):** A wealth of guides, tools, and funding resources.
- **LegalZoom / Rocket Lawyer:** For affordable legal documentation to establish your business entity.

To Begin Investing:

- **Vanguard, Fidelity, Charles Schwab:** Traditional brokers with extensive educational resources and low-cost investment options like index funds and ETFs.
- **M1 Finance, Betterment:** Modern platforms that combine investing with automated portfolio management (robo-advising).
- **Fundrise:** A platform for easily investing in real estate.

Enlisting the Experts: Learning from the Money Gurus

If managing your own finances feels daunting, you are not alone. There are qualified professionals whose job is to guide you.

- **Certified Public Accountant (CPA):** For tax strategy and preparation. (https://www.aicpa-cima.com/home)
- **Certified Financial Planner (CFP®):** For comprehensive financial planning, from retirement to estate planning. (https://www.letsmakeaplan.org)
- **Robo-Advisors:** Automated platforms like **Betterment** and **Wealthfront** that manage your investments for a low fee, perfect for beginners.

Conclusion: Your Journey to Financial Mastery

The path to financial independence begins with a decision to learn. Read the books, find the classics like **"The Richest Man in Babylon"** or **"Rich Dad Poor Dad"** on lists of best finance books. Invest time in your financial education as diligently as you invest time in your job. Remember, the goal is not just to earn more money, but to build a system where your money earns for you, granting you the ultimate asset: your time and freedom.

Chapter 8

The Illusion of Scarcity

Unmasking the True Nature of Money

& Breaking Free from The Rat Race

Introduction: The Endless Chase

We live in a world where some people worships at the altar of the almighty dollar. From a young age, we are conditioned to believe that the key to survival and success is to work harder, earn more, and accumulate as much of this paper and digital currency as possible. In America and across the globe, people are trading longer hours and immense energy for fiat currency, all in the desperate hope of securing a better life.

But what if everything we've been taught about money is a carefully constructed illusion? What if the very substance we chase so fervently is not what it seems? This chapter will pull back the curtain on the monetary system, revealing why we work so hard for something with no intrinsic value and how you can break free from this deception to build genuine, lasting wealth.

The Grand Deception: What is Money, Really?

For centuries, money was directly tied to something of tangible value, most famously gold and silver. This was known as the **"gold standard."** A dollar bill was essentially a receipt that could be exchanged for a specific amount of gold held in a vault. This link to a physical, finite commodity provided a natural check on how much money could be created.

However, in 1971, President Nixon severed the U.S. dollar's last link to gold. From that moment on, the global monetary system entered the era of **fiat currency**.

- **Fiat Money:** The word **"fiat"** comes from Latin, meaning **"let it be done**." Fiat currency has value simply because the government declares it to be legal tender and because society collectively agrees to believe in that value. It is not backed by any physical commodity like gold, oil, or real estate.
- **Backed by Debt:** In our current system, the vast majority of money is created when banks issue loans. When you take out a mortgage, the bank doesn't hand you a stack of existing cash; it creates new digital money in your account by entering numbers into a computer. This new money is literally created from debt. Your promise to repay the loan

(your debt) becomes the bank's asset, and the money in your account is a liability to the bank. The entire system is a complex web of IOUs.

Key Takeaway: The U.S. dollar is an IOU backed by nothing but faith and government mandate. Its value is an illusion sustained by collective belief, a belief that can be shattered during times of crisis.

The Puppeteers: The Federal Reserve and The Petro-Dollar

To understand the full picture, we must look at the architects of this system.

- **The Federal Reserve:** Contrary to its name, the Federal Reserve is not a federal agency. It is a unique, private-public hybrid entity created in 1913 by the Federal Reserve Act. While its Board of Governors is a government agency, the twelve regional Federal Reserve Banks are private corporations. Their immense power includes:
- **Controlling the Money Supply:** They decide how much money to print or create digitally.
- **Setting Interest Rates:** By raising or lowering rates, they dictate the cost of borrowing, influencing everything from your mortgage rate to car loans and business investments.
- **The Petro-Dollar System:** After leaving the gold standard, the U.S. struck a crucial deal with Saudi Arabia in the 1970s: the U.S. would provide military protection in exchange for Saudi Arabia pricing its oil exclusively in U.S. dollars. This created a massive, global demand for dollars, as every country needed them to buy the world's most critical commodity, oil. This system cemented the dollar's status as the world's primary reserve currency.

To learn more about this history, explore these resources:

- **Federal Reserve History: https://www.federalreservehistory.org**
- **The Balance - What is a Petro-Dollar: https://www.thebalancemoney.com/what-is-a-petrodollar-3306358**
- **Investopedia - Fiat Money: https://www.investopedia.com/terms/f/fiatmoney.asp**

The School of Conformity: How We Are Programmed to Be Employees, Not Owners

Our indoctrination begins in the very institutions meant to educate us. The standard public school curriculum, largely designed by government bodies, follows a clear, repetitive script:

1. Get good grades.
2. Go to a good college.
3. Get a **"good"** job (i.e., become a reliable employee for someone else's business).
4. Work hard for 40 years, hoping for raises and promotions.
5. Retire and hope your pension or 401(k) is enough.

Consider what was *never* on your syllabus:

- Did anyone teach you about **compound interest** and how it can make you wealthy over time?
- Were you shown how to analyze **dividend-paying stocks** that could provide passive income for life?
- Did your math classes cover the principles of **business startup, cash flow, or asset investment**?

This system is designed to produce compliant workers and eager consumers, not independent, critical-thinking wealth builders. It keeps you on the hamster wheel, where your primary function is to earn and immediately spend, fueling the very economy that depends on your perpetual participation.

Breaking the Cycle: From Consumer to Owner

The wealthy understand a fundamental secret: you don't get rich by spending your money; you get rich by having your money work for you. They use the system to their advantage.

- **The Spending Trap:** The moment the average person gets a raise, the conditioning kicks in. They upgrade their car, their house, their gadgets, increasing their lifestyle and expenses in lockstep with their income. This keeps them in a cycle of **"more money, more problems,"** with little to no wealth accumulation.
- **The Ownership Mindset:** The wealthy, conversely, use their income to acquire **assets**, things that put money *in* their pocket, like businesses, intellectual property, or income-generating real estate. They then use the cash flow from these assets to fund their lifestyle, breaking the link between their time and their money.

Do not fall into the consumer trap. Every dollar you spend on a liability is making someone else richer. Every dollar you channel into an asset is building your own fortress of wealth.

The Inevitable Crashes: Why the System is Inherently Unstable

Since the 2008 financial crisis, we have witnessed repeated economic turbulence. The stock market swings wildly, and the cost of living consistently rises, a phenomenon known as **inflation**.

Inflation is the silent thief of your labor. It erodes the purchasing power of every dollar you hold. A 3% annual inflation rate means that in 24 years, your dollar will only be worth about 50 cents today. When the system experiences a major crash, this process can accelerate into **hyperinflation**, where currency becomes nearly worthless, as seen in historical examples like Weimar Germany or, more recently, Zimbabwe and Venezuela.

Further Reading on Economic Vulnerability:

- **U.S. Bureau of Labor Statistics - Inflation Calculator:** https://www.bls.gov/data/inflation_calculator.htm

- **The Library of Economics and Liberty - Hyperinflation:** https://www.econlib.org/library/Enc/Hyperinflation.html

Your Path to Financial Sovereignty: Actionable Steps

You cannot control the global monetary system, but you can absolutely control your response to it. Here is how you can build a resilient financial life that is not entirely dependent on this fragile illusion.

1. **Flip the Script: Save to Invest.** Your first financial priority is not to spend, but to save with the explicit purpose of investing. Pay yourself first, aim to save a significant portion of every paycheck *before* you pay your bills or discretionary expenses.
2. **Invest in Tangible Assets.** Allocate a portion of your portfolio to **hard assets** that have stood the test of time. This includes gold and silver, which historically retain value when paper currencies falter.
3. **Become an Owner of Income-Producing Assets.**

- **Real Estate:** Purchase a rental property to generate passive income and benefit from appreciation.
- **Financial Markets:** Invest in low-cost index funds (like the S&P 500), dividend-paying stocks, or REITs (Real Estate Investment Trusts).
- **Your Own Business:** Start a side business or an online venture. In the digital age, the barriers to entry are lower than ever.

4. **Build a Fortress: Create an Emergency Fund.** Aim to save 3-6 months of living expenses in a secure, accessible account. This is your buffer against life's unexpected events and gives you the power to walk away from a toxic job or situation.
5. **Monetize What You Have:** Rent out a spare room, sell unused items, or freelance a skill. Every extra stream of income accelerates your journey to freedom.

Conclusion: Awakening to a New Reality

The deception of money is one of the most powerful forces shaping our modern lives. But once you see the illusion for what it is, you can no longer be fooled by it. True financial security does not come from a higher salary alone; it comes from owning a piece of the system itself.

Take complete ownership of your financial education and your future. Stop depending on a job or a government that operates within a fragile, debt-based system. Remember, the dollar is a tool, a useful one, but a tool nonetheless. Don't be the person who spends their life chasing the tool; be the architect who uses the tool to build a life of genuine, unshakeable wealth and freedom.

Chapter 9

Mastering Your Money

A Proven Blueprint to Spend Less and Save More

Introduction: The Nature of Money

We've all heard the saying, **"Money doesn't grow on trees."** For the vast majority of us, every dollar represents time, energy, and hard work. While there are a few primary ways people acquire money, such as inheritance, gifts, a steady paycheck, or business income, the most sustainable path to wealth is through your own efforts. This chapter isn't about how to *make* money, but about how to *keep* more of the money you make, building a foundation of financial security and freedom.

The Pillars of Financial Growth

Before we dive into daily habits, it's crucial to understand the three fundamental strategies for increasing your wealth. Your approach will depend on whether you're primarily an employee or a business owner.

1. **For the Business Owner: Expand and Invest.**
   If you run a business, your goal is to strategically increase your income. This can be done by **developing new revenue streams**, such as adding products or services that meet your customers' evolving needs. Additionally, you must transition from earning money solely through active work to making your money work for you. This means **professionally managing your business's profits** by investing in assets that appreciate or generate passive income, like dividend-paying stocks or bonds.
2. **For the Employee: Budget and Invest Wisely.**
   Your paycheck is your most valuable asset. The first step is to **create a workable budget** (more on this later) to control your cash flow. The second, and most critical step for long-term growth, is to channel your savings into **powerful investment vehicles**. This includes:

   - **Stocks & Bonds:** The building blocks of most investment portfolios.
   - **Mutual Funds and ETFs (Exchange-Traded Funds):** These allow you to invest in a diversified basket of stocks or bonds instantly, reducing risk.
   - **Real Estate:** This can be through direct ownership or more accessible methods like Real Estate Investment Trusts (REITs).

- **For Everyone: Leverage Legal Tax Advantages.**
  The government provides numerous incentives to save and invest. Don't leave this **"free money"** on the table. Key options include:
- **Real Estate:** The **1031 Exchange** allows you to defer capital gains taxes when selling an investment property and reinvesting the proceeds.
- **Retirement: Traditional IRAs** and **401(k)s** allow for tax-deferred growth, meaning you don't pay taxes until you withdraw the money.
- **Education: 529 Plans** offer tax-free growth for educational expenses.
- **Business:** If you have a side business or work from home, diligently research **home office deductions** and other business-related tax breaks.

Helpful Websites for Growth & Investing:

- https://www.investor.gov **(SEC):** A fantastic, unbiased resource for beginner investors.
- **NerdWallet:** Excellent for comparing brokerage accounts, IRAs, and credit cards.
- **The Balance:** Provides clear, in-depth articles on all aspects of personal finance and investing.

The Foundation: Controlling Your Spending

Understanding how to grow your money is futile if it's constantly leaking out due to poor spending habits. The two most significant obstacles to saving in America are:

1. **Lifestyle Inflation:** Living beyond your means by financing a life of luxury cars, overpriced homes, and consumer goods with high-interest debt.
2. **Crippling Debt:** The average American household carries significant debt from mortgages, auto loans, student loans, and credit cards, which drains bank accounts and creates a cycle of financial stress.

The only way to break this cycle is to take deliberate control of your spending habits. This starts with a realistic, detailed budget that tracks every dollar coming in and going out.

The 6-Step Blueprint to Save More Than You Spend

Here is your actionable plan to guarantee you will keep more of your hard-earned money each month.

1. Become a List Strategist.
Never go shopping, for groceries, clothes, or household goods, without a precise, pre-meditated list. Stores are scientifically designed to tempt you into impulse buys. A list is your shield. Stick to it relentlessly, and you will eliminate wasteful spending instantly.

2. Tame Recreational Spending.
Everyone deserves fun and relaxation, but this category can silently devour your budget. Allocate a specific, realistic amount for entertainment, dining out, vacations, and hobbies. Treat

this like any other necessary bill. Once the **"fun money"** is gone for the month, the free activities begin. This ensures your essential needs are always covered first.

3. Embrace the Power of Cash.
The psychology of spending with cash is fundamentally different than spending with plastic. When you use a credit card, you're spending abstract numbers. When you use cash, you physically see and feel the money leaving your hand. This tactile experience makes you more deliberate. For discretionary spending categories (like entertainment or personal shopping), try using the **"Cash Envelope System"**when the cash in the envelope is gone, you're done spending for the month.

4. Challenge the Brand Name Myth.
In many cases, generic or store-brand products are manufactured in the same facilities as name brands and are virtually identical in quality. Whether it's medication, groceries, or household items, opting for the generic version can save you 20-50%. Ask yourself: **"Am I buying this for its quality, or for its logo?"** Don't spend a premium just to impress others.

5. Build a Dynamic, Real-World Budget.
A budget isn't a punishment; it's a tool for freedom. It gives you permission to spend without guilt. Your budget must be detailed and include all categories:

- **Fixed Costs:** Rent/Mortgage, Car Payment, Insurance.
- **Variable Essentials:** Utilities, Groceries, Gas.
- **Financial Goals:** Savings, Investments, Debt Repayment.
- **Lifestyle:** Entertainment, Dining, Personal Care.

Helpful Websites for Budgeting:

- **https://mint.intuit.com :** A free, all-in-one platform that automatically tracks your spending and categorizes it for you.
- **You Need A Budget (YNAB):** A popular paid app that uses a proven methodology to **"Give every dollar a job."**

6. Automate Your Financial Integrity.
Paying bills late is like throwing cash in the trash. Late fees and reconnection charges are a complete waste of money. The simplest solution is to **automate your bill payments**. Set up automatic payments for all your fixed bills through your bank's bill pay service or directly with the service providers. For variable bills like utilities, you can often set up autopay for the minimum due to avoid a late fee, then pay the remainder manually.

Conclusion: Your Prosperous Future Awaits

Saving more than you spend requires mindfulness and discipline. It may mean making tough choices and sacrificing short-term wants for long-term security. But the reward is immense: reduced stress, the freedom to make life choices on your terms.

Chapter 10

Build Your Financial Freedom

A Practical Guide to Breaking the Debt Cycle

The American Debt Reality: You Are Not Alone

The financial struggle is real, and it's a burden shared by millions. Consider these sobering statistics that paint a clear picture of the challenge:

- The average American carries **$12,687** in personal debt from credit cards, auto loans, student loans, and other personal lines of credit.
- By the end of 2019, the total national consumer debt had ballooned to a staggering **$4.144 trillion**.
- More than **40 million Americans** live in poverty, defined as an annual income of less than **$24,563** for a family of four.
- A 2022 report revealed that **58% of Americans** have less than **$1,000** in savings to cover an unexpected emergency.

These numbers are more than just data; they represent a cycle of financial stress that feels inescapable for many. People work longer hours, yet their paychecks are consumed by debt payments and rising costs, leaving them right back where they started, or worse, further behind.

But this cycle *can* be broken. The path to financial stability isn't a secret reserved for the wealthy; it's a practical process of taking control. The time to change your future is now.

The Foundation: Your Three-Pillar Banking System

The first step to escaping the debt trap is to stop letting every dollar you earn disappear into a single account. You must become the commander of your cash. We do this by creating a simple, yet powerful, three-account system. This creates structure and purpose for every dollar you earn.

1. The Financial Firewall: Your Emergency Fund

This is your first and most important line of defense against life's surprises, a car repair, a medical bill, or a sudden job loss. Without this fund, any unexpected expense can force you deeper into debt.

- **Purpose:** To cover genuine emergencies, creating peace of mind and financial stability.

- **Funding Goal:** Start with a initial goal of **$1,000**, then build it to cover **3-6 months of essential living expenses**.
- **Key Strategy:** Keep this money in a separate, easily accessible savings account. Do not touch it for everyday spending or non-emergencies. Consistency is more important than the amount; automate a small transfer from every paycheck.

2. The Growth Engine: Your Investment Fund

This account is your vehicle for building future wealth. While your emergency fund protects you, your investment fund works for you, harnessing the power of compound interest.

- **Purpose:** To grow your wealth over the long term for retirement, major purchases, or financial independence.
- **Investment Vehicles:** There are many paths to growth. A few common ones include:

  Stocks & Bonds: Shares of companies or government/corporate debt.

  Mutual Funds & ETFs: Diversified baskets of stocks and/or bonds, perfect for beginners.

  Real Estate: Can provide both rental income and property value appreciation.

  Hard Assets & Digital Currency: Alternative investments like gold or Bitcoin (note: these are typically higher risk).

- **Key Strategy: Consult a Certified Financial Planner (CFP) or a fee-only financial advisor.** They can help you build a portfolio that matches your risk tolerance, timeline, and goals.

3. The Command Center: Your Living Expenses Account

This is the account from which you manage your daily life. It covers everything from rent and groceries to utilities and entertainment.

- **Purpose:** To fund your monthly living costs in a predictable controlled way.
- **Key Consideration:** Account for inflation, which historically increases the cost of living by about **2-3% per year**. This means your budget needs to be flexible and reviewed annually.
- **Funding:** This will likely be your largest account, typically requiring **50-60% of your take-home pay**.

Your Blueprint for Success: Crafting a Budget That Works

A budget isn't a restriction; it's a plan for your money. It's you telling your dollars where to go instead of wondering where they went. A successful budget is built on two principles: **awareness** and **intention**.

The 7 Steps to a Bulletproof Budget:

1. **Track Every Penny:** For one month, record every single income source and expense. Use a notebook, a spreadsheet, or a budgeting app. You can't manage what you don't measure.
    a. **Helpful Tool:** **https://mint.intuit.com** or **You Need A Budget (YNAB)** can automatically categorize your spending.
2. **Pay Yourself First:** Before you pay any bills, automatically divert a portion of your income, aim for at least **10%**, to your savings and investment accounts via direct deposit. This makes building wealth a non-negotiable habit.
3. **Categorize and Prioritize Spending:** Assign your remaining money to categories. A common guideline is the **50/30/20 rule**: 50% for Needs, 30% for Wants, and 20% for Savings/Debt. Adjust this to fit your reality, ensuring housing and utilities are covered first.
4. **Embrace the Power of Cash:** For categories where you tend to overspend (like groceries, dining, and entertainment), use the **"Cash Envelope System."** When the cash is gone, you stop spending. This creates a powerful physical connection to your money.
5. **Tackle High-Interest Debt Strategically:** Credit card interest is wealth's greatest enemy. Use either the **Debt Snowball** (paying off smallest debts first for psychological wins) or the **Debt Avalanche** (paying off highest-interest debts first to save money) method.
    a. **Helpful Tool:** **https://undebt.it** is a fantastic website for creating and tracking a debt payoff plan.
6. **Fortify Your Safety Net:** As you pay down debt, simultaneously build your emergency fund to its full 3-6 month target. This ensures a new emergency doesn't derail your progress.
7. **Commit to Living Within Your Means:** This is the cornerstone. It means spending less than you earn. It's not about deprivation, but about aligning your spending with your values and long-term goals.

Putting It All Together: A Sample Budget

Let's visualize a basic monthly budget for a take-home income of **$4,000**.

Income

Total Monthly Take-Home Pay	**$4,000**

Expenses

Income

Savings & Investments (20%)

Emergency Fund	$200	
Investment Fund	$600	
Living Expenses (60%)		
Rent/Mortgage	$1,200	
Utilities	$300	
Groceries	$400	
Transportation	$300	
Insurance	$200	
Lifestyle & Debt (20%)		
Dining & Entertainment	$300	
Personal Care	$100	
Debt Repayment	**$400**	
Total Expenses		**$4,000**

Your Journey to Financial Freedom

Breaking free from the debt cycle is a marathon, not a sprint. It requires a fundamental shift in your habits and mindset. Start today by creating a realistic budget that reflects your life. Then, establish your three-pillar banking system and begin funneling your money accordingly.

Be consistent, be patient, and regularly review your progress. As you monitor your spending, you will see your high-interest debts shrink and your savings and investments grow. This is the powerful shift from feeling controlled by money to being in command of it. This is your path to financial freedom.

Recommended Resources for Further Learning:

- **Budgeting Apps: Mint**, **You Need A Budget (YNAB)**, **PocketGuard**
- **Debt Paydown Tools:** https://undebt.it
- **Financial Education: NerdWallet**, **The Balance**, **The Simple Dollar**
- **Investing Basics:** https://www.sec.gov , https://www.investor.gov , https://www.bogleheads.org/blog/portfolio/the-bogleheads-guide-to-investing

Chapter 11

Taming the Debt Beast

From Financial Burden to Strategic Tool

Debt. For many, the word alone evokes a sense of dread, a heavy shadow that looms over daily life, silently draining bank accounts and siphoning away financial resources. The stress of out-of-control finances is real and pervasive. But what if you could shift your perspective and learn not just to escape debt, but to understand it? The journey to wealth isn't just about eliminating debt; it's about mastering its dual nature.

The American Debt Landscape

It's no secret that America runs on debt. Approximately 80% of Americans carry some form of debt, a burden that manifests as crushing student loans, towering credit card balances, expensive mortgages, and relentless medical and auto loans. This widespread debt isn't just a personal crisis; it's a national one, contributing to a sharp rise in financial bankruptcies across all demographics, from millennials just starting out to retirees who should be enjoying their golden years.

The Two Faces of Debt: Good vs. Bad

Understanding the fundamental difference between **"good"** and **"bad"** debt is the first step toward financial mastery. They are not created equal.

Good Debt: Leverage for Growth

Think of good debt as a strategic tool, much like a corporation does. It's not about borrowing to consume, but about borrowing to *invest*.

- **What it is:** Good debt is capital used to acquire something that has the potential to increase in value or generate long-term income. For a business, this means taking a loan to hire key staff, purchase efficient machinery, or expand into a new market. For an individual, this translates into:
- **A Mortgage:** A home is an asset that can appreciate over time.
- **Student Loans:** An investment in your education and earning potential.
- **A Business Loan:** Funding to start or scale a profitable venture.
- **The Mindset:** The savvy individual, like the smart businessperson, views this debt as **leverage**. It's a financial resource used to acquire an asset that would otherwise be

out of reach, ultimately accelerating wealth building. The return on investment (ROI) should, in theory, exceed the interest rate on the debt.

Bad Debt: The Wealth Killer

Bad debt is the opponent in your financial story. It funds depreciation and consumption, not appreciation.

What it is: This is money borrowed to purchase liabilities, items that lose value the moment you buy them and do not generate income. The most common and destructive examples include:

- **Credit Card Debt:** Often accrued for daily expenses, vacations, or consumer goods, with exorbitant interest rates.
- **Auto Loans:** Cars are notorious for rapidly depreciating in value.
- **Personal & Payday Loans:** Typically used to cover cash-flow shortfalls, these often come with predatory terms.

The Impact: Bad debt actively works against you. The problem is high interest compounds, creating a cycle where you're mostly paying off interest, not principal. This cripples your ability to save and invest, effectively robbing your future self of wealth.

Your Action Plan: Slaying the Dragon

Escaping the grip of bad debt requires a deliberate and empowered strategy. Here is your four-step battle plan.

1. Boost Your Income: Power Up Your Payments
Relying solely on a fixed paycheck to tackle high-interest debt can feel like running on a treadmill. You need to change the pace. Increasing your income gives you the extra firepower to attack your debt principal directly.

- **How to do it:** Seek a promotion, develop a marketable skill for freelance work (e.g., graphic design, coding, writing), or take on a side gig. As you mentioned, driving for Uber/Lyft, delivering food, or consulting in your field of expertise are all viable paths. The goal is to create a dedicated **"debt destruction"** fund from this new income.

2. Think Strategically: The Debt Avalanche Method
"Thinking outside the box" means adopting a proven, methodical approach to your repayment. We recommend the **Debt Avalanche** method, which you described perfectly.

- **How to do it:**

List Your Debts: Order all your bad debts from the highest interest rate to the lowest.

Pay Minimums: Continue making minimum payments on all debts.

Attack the Top: Throw every extra dollar from your budget and side income at the debt with the highest interest rate.

Snowball the Payments: Once the first debt is eliminated, roll the *entire* amount you were paying on it into the next debt on your list. This creates a powerful **"avalanche"** effect, speeding up the process as you go.

3. Master Your Money: The Non-Negotiable Budget
A budget is your map to freedom. It's not a restriction; it's a plan for your money to ensure every dollar has a purpose.

- **How to do it:** Use a simple spreadsheet or a budgeting app to track your income and every single expense. Categorize your spending to identify areas to cut back (e.g., dining out, subscriptions). Direct those savings straight to your debt avalanche. A realistic budget you can stick to is more valuable than a perfect one you abandon.

4. Celebrate the Milestones: Fuel Your Motivation
Paying off debt is a marathon, not a sprint. Acknowledging your progress is crucial for maintaining momentum.

- **How to do it:** When you pay off that first credit card or loan, **celebrate!** Mark the occasion with a low-cost or free reward, a picnic in the park, a movie night at home, a special meal you cook yourself. This positive reinforcement wires your brain to associate debt repayment with success. Remember, the goal is to celebrate your discipline, not to undermine it with new spending.

Helpful Resources on Your Journey

Budgeting & Tracking:

Mint (https://mint.intuit.com): A free, all-in-one tool to track spending, create budgets, and see all your accounts in one place.

You Need A Budget (YNAB) (https://www.ynab.com): A proactive budgeting method that gives every dollar a job. It's a paid subscription but is renowned for its effectiveness.

Debt Paydown Strategies & Support:

Undebt.it **(https://undebt.it):** A fantastic free tool that lets you simulate different payoff strategies (Avalanche vs. Snowball) and track your progress.

National Foundation for Credit Counseling (NFCC) (https://www.nfcc.org): A non-profit network that offers certified credit counseling and debt management plans, often for low or no cost.

Financial Education:

Consumer Financial Protection Bureau (CFPB) (https://www.consumerfinance.gov/complaint): A U.S. government agency providing a wealth of unbiased information on managing debt, credit cards, and loans.

Closing: Your Path to Financial Freedom

No one is meant to live in servitude to their debts. Finding yourself in debt is a situation; choosing to stay there is a choice. By understanding the nature of debt, creating a powerful plan, and using the right tools, you can slay the debt dragon. Celebrate each victory, protect your hard-won progress, and step forward into a future where you control your money, and your debt serves you, not the other way around. Your financial freedom is the ultimate prize.

Chapter 12

Charting Your Course

A Real-World Guide to Choosing a Career

One of the most defining decisions of your life is choosing a career path. It can feel like an immense pressure, especially when you're young and your resume is filled with potential rather than experience. How can you possibly know what you'll want to do for the next 10, 20, or 40 years? The truth is, you aren't expected to have all the answers right away, but with a strategic approach, you can make an informed and confident choice.

The Influences That Shape Our Path

For many, our early career ideas are heavily shaped by our environment. Parents are often the most significant influence, sometimes gently guiding and other times strongly steering their children toward professions they value. This can be a wonderful source of wisdom, but it can also lead to a conflict if your passions lie elsewhere.

Furthermore, your geographic location and socioeconomic background play a crucial role. The opportunities available in a small rural town differ greatly from those in a major metropolitan city. For students from working-class or low-income families, the dream of an expensive, private university might seem out of reach, but it's critical to know that this does not close the door on a successful and fulfilling career.

The Modern Career Landscape: It's Okay to Pivot

The old idea of a **"job for life"** is fading. Statistics show that the average person will change careers, not just jobs, between **3 and 7 times** during their working life. This is driven by rapid advancements in technology, artificial intelligence, and a constantly evolving economy. This isn't a sign of failure; it's a reflection of a dynamic world and our own personal growth.

When evaluating a potential career, it's wise to consider two key factors for long-term stability:

1. **Longevity and Future-Proofing:** Is this a field with a strong outlook? Will it be relevant in 10 or 20 years? Look for careers that are resistant to automation and aligned with future societal needs, like healthcare, renewable energy, or data science.
2. **Financial Viability and Growth:** Does this career offer a genuine living wage with clear pathways for advancement? You need a career that can support your desired lifestyle and provide financial security.

Your Toolkit for Career Discovery

Thankfully, you don't have to navigate this journey alone. A wealth of online resources can provide data-driven insights to inform your decision.

Career Exploration and Self-Assessment:

https://www.onetonline.org : Sponsored by the U.S. Department of Labor, this is the ultimate database for detailed information on hundreds of occupations, including tasks, skills, required education, and job outlook.

https://www.mynextmove.org : A user-friendly site built on O*NET data, perfect for exploring careers by keyword, industry, or by answering questions about your interests.

https://www.careerplanner.com : As mentioned, this site offers a vast list of over 12,000 careers with details on education, salary, and work environment.

Job Market Research and Practical Advice:

https://www.bls.gov/ooh : This is the gold standard for unbiased government data on job growth, median pay, and entry-level education requirements.

https://www.thebalancemoney.com/career-planning-4161513 : An excellent resource for practical advice on resumes, interviewing, salary negotiation, and career planning from industry experts.

Education and Training Pathways:

https://www.collegechoice.net : A great site for researching and comparing different academic programs and their potential returns.

Navigating Real-World Obstacles

What if your dream path seems blocked by financial or environmental constraints? Here are four powerful and proven alternative pathways to a successful career:

1. **The Military Option:** The Army, Navy, Air Force, Marines, Coast Guard, and Space Force offer extensive training, educational benefits (like the GI Bill), and a chance to develop unparalleled discipline and skills.
2. **The Community College Route:** An affordable, **"pay-as-you-go"** option to complete general education requirements, earn an associate degree, or receive specific career training without the burden of excessive student debt.
3. **Vocational or Trade School:** These programs focus on high-demand, skilled trades such as Electrician, Plumbing, HVAC Technician, Welding, or Carpentry. These careers often offer excellent pay, job security, and the satisfaction of hands-on work.

4. **Entrepreneurship:** Starting your own business is the ultimate path of self-reliance. It requires immense dedication, but it allows you to build something that is entirely your own.

The Final Compass: Aligning Passion with Practicality

You will often hear the advice, **"Follow your passion."** While this is ideal, a more balanced approach is often more sustainable. A better strategy is to **find the intersection between what you're good at, what the world needs, and what you can get paid for.**

Start with a career that leverages your strengths and provides financial stability. Use that security as a foundation to explore your passions, whether through hobbies, side projects, or eventually transitioning into a field that combines both income and interest. The sweet spot is finding a career you are genuinely interested in that also offers an excellent income and growth potential.

In Closing, choosing a career is a journey of self-discovery, not a single decision made in a day. Be patient with yourself. Invest time in learning who you are, your skills, interests, and values. Then, research the opportunities that align with that identity. Your first choice does not have to be your last, but a thoughtful, informed choice will set you on a strong and promising path forward.

Chapter 13

The Innovator and The Architect

Building a Business with Creativity and Craft

Introduction

Is a brilliant, disruptive idea enough to build a legendary company? Or is it meticulous planning and specialized knowledge that truly lays the foundation for success? This chapter explores the two powerful, often seemingly opposed, forces that drive business creation and growth: the visionary **Innovator** (the creative mind) and the strategic **Architect** (the educated mind).

We will delve into the unique strengths of each mindset, examining iconic examples of those who thrived primarily through raw creativity and those who rely on structured education. Ultimately, we will answer the central question: Must you choose a side, or is the chemistry of both the true secret to building a lasting enterprise?

The Innovator: Seeing the World Anew

Creativity is more than just artistic expression; in business, it is the engine of innovation. It's the ability to connect contrasting dots, to envision a solution to a problem no one has articulated, and to imagine a future that doesn't yet exist. It's the birthplace of the **"what if."**

Other names for this mindset: Inventiveness, Imagination, Innovation, Vision, Ingenuity, Resourcefulness.

The most compelling case for the creative mind often comes from the stories of legendary college dropouts who redefined entire industries. Their success wasn't rooted in a diploma but in a relentless focus on a novel idea.

- **Steve Jobs** (Apple): Championed the intersection of technology and the liberal arts, insisting that powerful technology must be intuitive and beautiful.
- **Mark Zuckerberg** (Facebook): Saw the potential for a connected social network from his dorm room, prioritizing growth and user experience over traditional business formalities.
- **Jan Koum** (WhatsApp): Built a simple, ad-free messaging service focused on user privacy, disrupting the telecom industry.
- **Travis Kalanick** (Uber): Reimagined urban transportation by leveraging smartphone technology, creating the **"ride-sharing"** model.

These Innovators understood that a degree is a tool, not the destination. They prove that a powerful vision, when executed with passion and resilience, can generate immense value that far exceeds the credential of a diploma. The Innovator asks, **"Why not?"**

Deepen Your Understanding:

- **TED Talk: "*How to Build Your Creative Confidence*"** by David Kelley
- **Book: "*The Innovator's Dilemma*"** by Clayton M. Christensen
- **Website: Fast Company (https://www.fastcompany.com)** - A leading media brand focused on innovation in technology, leadership, and design.

The Architect: Building on a Foundation of Knowledge

If the Innovator paints the vision, the Architect draws the blueprints. The educated mind brings discipline, structure, and specialized expertise. This mindset is characterized by a deep understanding of systems, processes, and established knowledge. It turns a visionary idea into a operational, scalable, and sustainable business.

- **Other names for this mindset:** Knowledgeable, Analytical, Strategic, Methodical, Expert.

There are fields where formal education is not just beneficial but non-negotiable. We rightly demand that our surgeons, aerospace engineers, and structural architects be highly trained and certified. Similarly, in business, the complex machinery of finance, legal compliance, supply chain logistics, and data analysis requires an Architect's touch.

Businesses like **SpaceX** and **Tesla**, while driven by a visionary (Elon Musk), are utterly dependent on thousands of highly educated engineers, physicists, and programmers to turn sci-fi concepts into reality. The Architect ensures the rocket not only inspires us but also safely reaches orbit. The Architect asks, **"How, and how sustainably?"**

Deepen Your Understanding:

- **Online Learning: Coursera (https://www.coursera.org)** or **edX (https://www.edx.org)** - Offer courses and specializations in business fundamentals from top universities.
- **Book: "*The Personal MBA: Master the Art of Business*"** by Josh Kaufman
- **Resource: SCORE (https://www.score.org)** - Provides free mentorship and templates for business plans, financial projections, and marketing strategy.

The False Dichotomy: Why You Need Both

Framing this as a battle, creativity vs. education, is a dangerous oversimplification. The most successful and enduring companies are not built by one or the other, but through a symbiotic relationship between the two.

- **The Idea is Nothing Without Execution:** A revolutionary idea for a social network is just a daydream without the educated understanding of database architecture, user interface design, and server management to build it.
- **Execution is Directionless Without Vision:** A flawless business plan and a perfect supply chain are worthless if the product they support is a mediocre, **"me-too"** offering that no one wants.

Consider the companies you listed:

- **Amazon** began with Jeff Bezos's creative insight into the potential of online commerce (the Innovator). It was scaled into a global behemoth through relentless focus on data, logistics, and operational excellence (the Architects).
- **Apple** is the quintessential example. Steve Jobs provided the creative vision and uncompromising design ethos, while Tim Cook, an operational expert, built the supremely efficient supply chain that made that vision profitable on a global scale.

The Uncontrollable Variable: Timing and Luck

Even with a perfect blend of innovation and education, there are no guarantees in business. Timing and market readiness are wild cards. A brilliant idea launched during an economic recession may struggle to find funding. A product ahead of its time may fail, only for a similar one to succeed years later when the culture and technology have caught up (e.g., tablet computers before the iPad). The key is to research your market relentlessly and be prepared to adapt.

Your Path Forward: Cultivating a Complete Mindset

You may naturally lean more toward being an Innovator or an Architect. The goal is not to fundamentally change who you are, but to consciously develop the muscles you lack.

1. **If You're an Innovator:** Dedicate time to learning business fundamentals. Understand a balance sheet, study marketing funnels, and learn the basics of operational management. Your ideas will become more viable and investable.
2. **If You're an Architect:** Actively create space for creativity and **"blue-sky thinking."** Challenge your own assumptions, seek diverse perspectives, and practice brainstorming without judgment. This will help you identify new opportunities for growth and innovation.

Conclusion: The Symphony of Success

In the end, the question is not whether the creative mind is better than the educated mind, or vice versa. The question is how to orchestrate them in harmony.

The **Innovator** composes the melody, the inspiring, memorable idea that captures hearts and minds. The **Architect** writes the score, the detailed arrangement that allows an orchestra to play that melody beautifully and consistently. A business with only a melody is a fleeting tune. A business with only a score is silent.

Invest in your people, value both sets of skills, and foster an environment where creative vision and educated execution are not at odds, but are partners in the shared mission of building something truly great. Your business's success depends on this vital collaboration.

Chapter 14

The Self Starter's Blueprint

Launching Your Venture with Minimal Capital

Introduction: Is "No Money Down" Really Possible?

The dream of starting a business often collides with the hard reality of startup costs. But what if the dream doesn't have to die at the hands of an empty bank account? Is it truly possible to start a real business with no money?

The resounding answer is **Yes!**

However, we must reframe what **"no money**" means. While you may not need a massive amount of liquid capital, you will always invest something of value, your time, your skills, or your existing assets. The key is to leverage non-financial resources to generate the momentum and capital you need.

This chapter will guide you through the mindset and methods to get your business off the ground by creatively using what you already have.

The Foundation: Three Zero-Capital Starting Points

Before we explore ways to *generate* capital, let's look at three scenarios where you can acquire or begin a business with virtually no cash out-of-pocket.

1. **The Inheritance Path.** You inherit an operational business from a family member or friend. This is a direct transfer of an existing entity with products, services, and a customer base. While rare, it's a clear example of a business started with no personal capital.
2. **The Gifted Opportunity.** Someone gifts you their business, perhaps because they are retiring or pursuing a new path. This is similar to an inheritance but can happen outside of family ties. It requires being in the right place at the right time and having the trust of the current owner.
3. **The Skill-Based Launchpad.** This is the most accessible and controllable path for the vast majority of aspiring entrepreneurs. **You use your high-demand skills to generate the initial capital for your business.** This isn't just **"starting a business";** it's *funding* it through your own expertise.

Example: A software developer takes on freelance projects after hours to fund their dream of creating a SaaS (Software-as-a-Service) product.

Example: An auto mechanic uses weekend jobs to save up for their own garage, turning a side hustle into the seed money for the main venture.

If Option 3 is your path, be prepared for hard work. You are essentially running two jobs, your day job and your funding engine, but the reward is building a business on your own terms, debt-free.

The Modern Self Starter's Toolkit: 7 Ways to Fund Your Dream

If you're building from the ground up, you'll need resources. Here are seven proven methods to generate the capital you need without taking on debilitating debt.

1. Leverage Your Own Future: The 401(k) Loan

If you have a 401(k) through your employer, you may be able to borrow against it. The beauty of this method is that you're paying the interest back to *yourself*.

- **Key Considerations:** Loan limits are typically 50% of your vested balance up to $50,000. You must repay it with interest (to yourself) through payroll deductions, usually within 5 years. **Crucially, if you leave your job, the loan often becomes due in full, which can be a significant risk.**
- **Action Step:** Speak with your 401(k) plan administrator to understand the specific terms, interest rates, and risks involved.

2. The Strategic Side Hustle

A second job is a time-tested way to raise capital quickly. The modern "gig economy" offers unprecedented flexibility.

- **Beyond Driving:** While Uber, Lyft, and food delivery are popular, also consider skill-based gigs on platforms like **Upwork** or **Fiverr**. If you're a writer, designer, or programmer, you can earn startup funds while honing the very skills your future business will use.

Resource Links:

https://www.upwork.com - For freelance professional services.

https://www.fiverr.com - To offer "gigs" based on your skills.

https://www.taskrabbit.com - For local handyman and odd jobs.

Rover - For pet sitting and dog walking.
https://www.rover.com/?_gl=1*nb73uc*_up*MQ..*_gs*MQ..&gclid=CjwKCAiAwqHIBhAEEiwAx9cTeTKTn4vbUZDyrEGbvMhXSEzChe_75mPZ0hqu0BAkig7Pa_wLnJw1NhoCS9MQAvD_BwE&gbraid=0AAAAADPp_a4y7zxJIreM9_KVPdHKcQrLt

3. Crowdfunding: Pre-Sell Your Vision

Crowdfunding allows you to raise small amounts of money from a large number of people, typically via online platforms. There are two main types:

- **Rewards-Based:** Backers receive a product or perk in return for their pledge (e.g., a pre-order of your new gadget). This is excellent for product-based businesses.
- **Equity-Based:** Backers receive a small stake in your company. This is more complex and regulated but can raise significant capital.
- **Resource Links:**

  https://www.kickstarter.com/?ref=nav - The leader in rewards-based funding for creative projects.

  https://www.indiegogo.com/en - Offers both flexible and fixed funding models.

  https://www.startengine.com & **https://wefunder.com** - Leading platforms for equity crowdfunding.

4. Monetize Your Clutter: The Asset Liquidation Sale

The old adage, **"one person's trash is another's treasure,"** is a powerful funding tool. Host a garage sale or use online marketplaces to sell items you no longer need.

- **Maximize Your Return:** Don't just stick to a driveway sale. Use **Facebook Marketplace**, **eBay**, and **OfferUp** to reach a wider audience for higher-value items like electronics, collectibles, or brand-name clothing.
- **Action Step:** Dedicate a weekend to gathering, pricing, and selling. Every dollar earned is a dollar invested in your dream.

5. Partner with Investors

If you have a scalable idea and a solid plan, you can seek funding from angels or venture capitalists (VCs). They provide capital in exchange for equity and often bring valuable mentorship and connections.

- **The Prerequisite:** You must have a **bulletproof business plan** and a compelling pitch. Investors are looking for high-growth potential and a strong return on their investment (ROI).
- **Resource Links:**

https://wellfound.com - A major network for startups to connect with angel investors.

https://gust.com - A platform used by startups and investors to manage the investment process.

https://www.startengine.com/seedinvest - A curated equity crowdfunding platform for serious startups.

6. The Family and Friends Round

Borrowing from loved ones is a traditional method, but it comes with significant emotional risk.

- **Best Practices: Treat it professionally.** Create a formal written agreement that outlines the loan amount, interest rate, repayment schedule, and what happens if the business fails. This protects both your finances and your relationships.
- **Action Step:** Be transparent about the risks and have a clear plan for how you will succeed. Never assume it's **"just family money."**

7. Government and Institutional Support: The SBA

The U.S. Small Business Administration (SBA) is an invaluable resource. While they don't give grants to start a typical small business, they **guarantee loans** made by partner lenders, reducing the risk for banks and making it easier for you to qualify.

- **Key Programs:**

  7(a) Loans: The most common type for general business purposes.

  Microloans: Smaller loans up to $50,000, perfect for very small startups.

  Small Business Investment Companies (SBICs): Privately owned funds that the SBA licenses to provide venture capital and financing.

- **Essential Resource:** Your first stop should be the https://www.sba.gov . Use their free learning platforms, https://learning.sba.gov , and their local https://www.score.org mentorship program for guidance.

Your Launch Sequence: A Plan for Action

Success is not found in a single funding method but in a disciplined, multi-step approach.

1. **Craft Your Business Plan First.** You cannot attract funding, whether from an investor, the SBA, or your family, without a clear, written plan. It is your roadmap and your sales document.

2. **Choose Your Funding Strategy.** Will you bootstrap with a side hustle? Pre-sell via crowdfunding? Pursue an SBA-backed loan? Your business type and goals will determine the best path. Many successful founders use a combination of these methods.
3. **Execute with Relentless Action.** Ideas are worthless without execution. The **"hard work"** you put in on weekends or after hours is the down payment on your future freedom.

4. The path to entrepreneurship without a large bankroll is challenging but profoundly rewarding. You are forced to be resourceful, lean, and deeply connected to your customers from day one. Don't wait for the "**perfect"** moment or a lottery win. Start where you are, use what you have, and begin building your future today.

Chapter 15

Fortifying Your Venture

A Practical Guide to Business Resilience & Contingency Planning

Introduction: The Dual Reality of Entrepreneurship

There is an amazing thrill in starting your own business, a feeling of empowerment and freedom as you step into the role of your own boss and take control of your financial destiny. This drive for autonomy is a powerful motivator. However, this excitement is often tempered by a sobering reality: the statistics for new business survival are intimidating.

Before getting swept away by the initial excitement, it's crucial to understand the landscape. Approximately **20% of small businesses fail within their first year**, and by the end of their fifth year, roughly **50% have closed their doors** (U.S. Bureau of Labor Statistics). With over 30 million small businesses in the U.S., these numbers represent a significant number of entrepreneurial dreams that face challenges.

This chapter isn't meant to discourage you, but to empower you. By understanding why businesses fail and proactively building a resilient operation, you can dramatically increase your odds of becoming a success story.

The Top Reasons Businesses Fail: Learning from Others' Mistakes

Why do so many ventures falter? The reasons are often interconnected, but several common themes emerge:

1. **Insufficient Capital & Cash Flow Crises:** Running out of money is the number one killer. Many entrepreneurs underestimate their startup costs and overestimate how quickly revenue will arrive. It's not just about the initial investment; it's about having enough room to survive the tough early months.
2. **Lack of Market Demand:** A brilliant idea is worthless if no one is willing to pay for it. This failure stems from not validating the business idea with the target audience beforehand.
3. **Excessive Overhead & Poor Financial Management:** High fixed costs, like expensive office space or oversized inventory, can sink a business during a slow period. Without diligent financial oversight, expenses can quickly spiral out of control.

4. **Overwhelming Competition & Irrelevance:** Failing to understand your competition or differentiate your offering leads to irrelevance. Your product or service must have a clear value proposition that sets it apart.
5. **Legal Challenges & Regulatory Issues:** Unexpected lawsuits, intellectual property disputes, or failure to comply with regulations can incur massive, unforeseen costs.
6. **An Inadequate or Nonexistent Business Plan:** A business without a plan is like a ship without a rudder. The plan forces you to think through your strategy, finances, and market, revealing potential pitfalls before you commit.

A less critical, but common, reason for closure is owner retirement or burnout, especially when there is no succession plan in place.

Building a Fortress: Proactive Strategies to Keep Your Business Operational

Success is not about avoiding problems, but about being prepared for them. Here's how to build a resilient business from the ground up.

1. Conduct Rigorous Pre-Launch Due Diligence

Before you invest a dollar, answer these foundational questions:

- **Product/Market Fit:** How well do my products or services solve a real problem or fulfill a desire for my target customers? Conduct surveys and gather feedback.
- **Competitive Analysis:** Who are my direct and indirect competitors? What are they doing well? What can I do better, cheaper, or differently? Perform a SWOT (Strengths, Weaknesses, Opportunities, Threats) analysis.
- **Economic Resilience:** How would my business withstand an economic downturn? Do I have a lean enough model to survive a recession? Consider creating multiple financial forecasts (optimistic, pessimistic, realistic).

2. Develop a Living, Breathing Contingency Plan

A contingency plan is your playbook for when things go wrong. It should address the critical vulnerabilities we discussed:

- **Cash Flow Shortfall:** Maintain an emergency fund (often 3-6 months of operating expenses) and establish a line of credit *before* you need it.
- **Wrong Team Dynamics:** Hire for attitude and cultural fit as much as for skill. Have clear performance metrics and be willing to make difficult personnel changes.
- **Shifting Market Prices:** Regularly review your pricing strategy. Can you offer different tiers of service? What value can you add to justify your price?
- **Customer Dissatisfaction:** Implement a robust system for collecting and acting on customer feedback. A happy customer is a repeat customer; an unhappy one can damage your reputation.
- **Ineffective Marketing:** Track your marketing ROI meticulously. Be prepared to pivot your strategy if certain channels aren't working. The goal is a consistent stream of new leads.

- **Legal & Operational Emergencies:** Consult with a business attorney to understand your risks. Consider appropriate business insurance (liability, property, etc.).

Key Pillars for Long-Term Operational Health

Once you're operational, your focus must shift to sustainability.

- **The Power of Your Business Plan:** Your business plan is not a static document to be filed away. Revisit and revise it quarterly. It is your strategic compass, keeping you aligned with your goals and adaptable to change.
- **Prudent Financial Management:** Keep your fixed expenses as low as possible. Scrutinize every cost. Use accounting software to monitor your cash flow daily and understand your key financial metrics (e.g., gross margin, burn rate).
- **Customer-Centricity is Everything:** Your customers pay the bills. Foster loyalty through exceptional service, actively seek their input, and make them feel valued. A strong reputation is your best marketing.
- **Prioritize Strategic Growth:** Stagnation is a precursor to failure. Continuously look for ways to expand your sales, introduce new products or services, and enter new markets. Sustainable growth is a deliberate process.

Facing the Unthinkable: A Graceful Exit or Pivot

Even with the best planning, sometimes a business model proves unviable. Recognizing this early is a sign of strength, not failure.

- **The Pivot:** Can you change your product, target market, or revenue model to better meet market demands? Many successful companies, like Slack (which started as a gaming company), are the result of a strategic pivot.
- **The Orderly Wind-Down:** If closure is the only option, do it professionally.

- **Notify Stakeholders:** Communicate transparently with employees, customers, and suppliers.
- **Fulfill Obligations:** Settle debts with creditors to the best of your ability.
- **Formal Dissolution:** File the necessary paperwork with your state to legally dissolve the business entity.
- **Seek Professional Advice:** A lawyer or accountant can guide you through this process to minimize legal and financial repercussions.

Conclusion: Your Journey to a Resilient Business

Starting a business is a courageous endeavor that is neither easy nor guaranteed. However, by replacing fear with preparation, you can navigate the challenges. Your success hinges on a solid plan, a vigilant eye on your finances, an unwavering focus on your customers, and the flexibility to adapt when necessary.

Start today. Begin building not just a business, but a resilient enterprise capable of weathering storms and seizing opportunities. Your proactive planning is the most valuable investment you will ever make.

Additional Resources and Helpful Websites

- **U.S. Small Business Administration (SBA):** `www.sba.gov`

The definitive resource for entrepreneurs. Offers free business planning templates, guides on financing, local assistance, and counseling (through SCORE and Small Business Development Centers).

- **SCORE:** `www.score.org`

Provides free, confidential mentorship from experienced business professionals and a vast library of workshops and webinars.

- **Nolo – Legal Guides for Small Business:** `www.nolo.com`

An excellent source for understanding legal basics, from forming an LLC to creating contracts and understanding employment law.

- **QuickBooks Blog (Intuit):** `https://quickbooks.intuit.com/r/`

A fantastic resource for articles on accounting, cash flow management, tax tips, and overall small business financial health.

- **Harvard Business Review – Entrepreneurship Section:** `https://hbr.org/topic/entrepreneurship`

For strategic insights, case studies, and deep dives into business growth, leadership, and innovation.

Chapter 16

Fortifying Your Finances

A Practical Guide to Economic Resilience

Navigating a World of Financial Uncertainty

We are living in an era of profound global economic uncertainty. From the streets of American cities to the markets of Europe and Asia, a complex web of pressures threatens the financial security of individuals and families. Acknowledging these risks is not an act of fear, but the first step toward empowerment and protection.

Let's examine some of the key issues impacting our financial landscape:

- **Soaring Government Debt:** The U.S. national debt has surpassed **$38 trillion**, a staggering burden that creates long-term economic vulnerability and can lead to higher taxes or reduced government services. (Source: U.S. Treasury Department)
- **Geopolitical Instability:** Tensions with global powers like China and Russia, along with ongoing conflicts, disrupt supply chains, fuel energy price volatility, and create unpredictable market swings.
- **Social and Economic Strain:** Rising unemployment, layoffs in key sectors, and increasing poverty rates contribute to social unrest and higher crime in many communities.
- **Market Volatility:** The stock and bond markets are on a rollercoaster, influenced by fluctuating interest rates set by the Federal Reserve to combat inflation.
- **The Silent Tax of Inflation:** While the rate may fluctuate, the cumulative effect of inflation drastically erodes purchasing power. The cost of essentials like food, housing, and healthcare continues to outpace wage growth for many.
- **The Tax Burden:** State and local governments frequently adjust sales and property taxes to meet budgets, directly impacting your disposable income.

These are not abstract concepts; they are real forces that can directly impact your job, your savings, and your family's well-being.

The Expert Outlook: A Call for Caution

The consensus among many leading economists and financial institutions is sobering. They warn of a significant potential for a global economic downturn or **"meltdown,"** potentially more severe than the 2008-2009 financial crisis. The causes they cite are systemic:

- **Unprecedented Debt Levels:** Governments worldwide are financing their operations through massive deficits.
- **Quantitative Easing (QE) Aftermath:** The trillions of dollars injected into the economy post-2008 and during the COVID-19 pandemic have inflated asset prices and contributed to the inflation we see today.

The 2008 crisis decimated the middle class, wiping out home equity and retirement accounts overnight. Experts suggest the next crisis could have a similar, if not greater, impact, underscoring the critical need for personal preparedness.

The Double-Edged Sword: Technology and AI

Beyond traditional economic threats, the rapid rise of technology presents a fundamental shift. The deployment of 5G and, more significantly, the integration of Artificial Intelligence (AI) and automation will reshape the workforce. Studies, including those from the **McKinsey Global Institute**, estimate that by 2030, **up to 30% of hours worked today could be automated**.

This transition threatens to displace millions in low-to-mid-skilled roles, from drivers and cashiers to administrative staff. This large-scale job displacement could exacerbate unemployment and social instability, making individual adaptation more critical than ever.

Your Action Plan: Building a Fortress of Financial Resilience

Understanding the risks is only half the battle. The other half is taking decisive, proactive steps to protect yourself. Here are three pillars of personal economic resilience:

1. Proactive Planning, Not Panic

Waiting for a crisis to hit is a recipe for disaster. The time to fortify your position is now, while the sun is still shining.

- **Conduct a "Job Security" Audit:** Is your role vulnerable to automation, outsourcing, or industry downturns? If so, what skills can you acquire now to make yourself indispensable or pivot to a more resilient field?
- **Stress-Test Your Finances:** If the stock market dropped 40% tomorrow, how would your retirement savings look? If you lost your job, how long could you survive? Answering these questions honestly reveals your vulnerabilities.

Resource:

- **The Bureau of Labor Statistics (BLS) Occupational Outlook Handbook:** This is an excellent tool to research which careers are projected to grow or decline over the next decade. https://www.bls.gov/ooh

2. Cultivate a Global and Entrepreneurial Mindset

The digital economy has erased borders. Your potential customer base is the entire online world. A **"side hustle"** is no longer just for extra cash; it can be a vital lifeline and a source of diversified income.

- **Identify a Niche:** What knowledge, skill, or product do you have that can serve a global audience? This could be digital products, online coaching, freelance writing, or e-commerce.
- **Build Your Digital Presence:** Start a website, a professional social media profile, or a store on a platform like Etsy or Shopify. The barrier to entry has never been lower.

Resources:

- **Skillshare / Coursera:** Platforms to learn high-income, digitally-focused skills like digital marketing, coding, or graphic design.
- **Shopify Blog:** A wealth of free information on starting and running an online business. **https://www.shopify.com/blog**

3. Master Your Cash Flow and Fortify with an Emergency Fund

This is the cornerstone of financial security. An emergency fund is your personal buffer against life's inevitable shocks, from a job loss to a major car repair.

- **The Golden Standard:** Strive to save **3-6 months' worth of essential living expenses**. If you are in a volatile industry or are a single-income household, aim for 9-12 months.
- **Make it Automatic:** Set up an automatic transfer from your checking to a dedicated high-yield savings account immediately after each payday. Treat this transfer as a non-negotiable bill.

Resources:

- **NerdWallet or Bankrate:** These sites are excellent for comparing the best high-yield savings accounts to ensure your emergency fund earns as much interest as possible.
- **Your Local Credit Union:** Often offer great rates on savings accounts and can provide personalized financial counseling.

Conclusion: Your Economy, Your Responsibility

We cannot control the global economy, geopolitical tensions, or the pace of technological change. But we can control our response. The power to build a resilient financial life lies in your hands. By planning proactively, thinking entrepreneurially, and securing your financial foundations, you transform anxiety into action. Start today. The peace of mind that comes from being properly protected is the greatest asset you will ever own.

Chapter 17

Financial Resilience

A Strategic Guide to Avoiding Business Failure

& Navigating Bankruptcy

Introduction: The True Nature of Financial Crisis

Bankruptcy is a word that strikes fear into the heart of any business owner or individual. While avoiding it should be a primary goal, it's crucial to understand that financial distress is often a symptom of a deeper issue, not the problem itself. The uncertainty of the economy can expose underlying weaknesses, but it doesn't have to be the end of your story. For many, a financial crisis, or even bankruptcy, can become a painful but valuable lesson, providing a clean slate and the momentum to rebuild on a stronger foundation.

The core insight is this: people and businesses don't typically fail because of a single, catastrophic money problem. They fail due to a **lack of financial literacy and management skills**. Throwing more money at a financial literacy problem is like trying to put out a fire with gasoline. The solution isn't more capital; it's more knowledge.

Part 1: The Personal Foundation - Building Your Financial Literacy

Before you can save a business, you must understand money. The principles of personal finance are the bedrock upon which all successful businesses are built.

Shifting Your Mindset: From Spender to Manager
The first step is a mental shift. You must stop viewing money as a temporary tool for paying bills and start seeing it as a resource to be managed, grown, and invested. Many working-class individuals and entrepreneurs exacerbate their problems by trying to solve financial shortfalls with more debt or risky **"quick fixes,"** which is essentially gambling. The problem persists until the root cause, financial illiteracy, is addressed.

The Education Advantage: It's Not About Your Salary
Consider the financial stability of professionals like doctors, lawyers, and engineers. While high incomes help, their real advantage is often their highly specialized, negotiable skill set. This translates to greater control over their earning potential. The principle is universal: **the more valuable your skills, the more financial control you command.** The good news is that you don't need an expensive degree to acquire these skills.

Your Self-Education Toolkit: Books and Online Resources
The internet and bookstores have democratized financial education. For the price of a few cups of coffee, you can access world-class knowledge.

Recommended Books:

- **"Rich Dad Poor Dad" by Robert Kiyosaki:** Challenges your perspective on assets and liabilities.
- **"The Total Money Makeover" by Dave Ramsey:** A proven, step-by-step plan for getting out of debt.
- **"The Intelligent Investor" by Benjamin Graham:** The bible for value investing, teaching a disciplined, long-term approach.
- **"Profit First" by Mike Michalowicz:** A revolutionary system for business accounting that ensures profitability from day one.

Informative Websites & Platforms:

- **For Personal Finance & Investing:**

The Simple Dollar (https://thesimpledollar.com **)**: Offers practical advice on budgeting, saving, and investing.

NerdWallet (https://www.nerdwallet.com): Provides comparisons for credit cards, bank accounts, loans, and brokerages.

- **For Investment Education:**

Investopedia (https://investopedia.com)An extensive dictionary and educational resource for all things finance and investing.

Babypips (https://www.babypips.com): An excellent, free resource for learning the basics of forex and crypto trading.

- **For Automated Investing:**

Betterment (https://www.betterment.com)
& **Wealthfront** (https://www.wealthfront.com): Robo-advisors that build and manage a diversified portfolio for you based on your goals.

Part 2: The Business Blueprint - Ensuring Your Company Survives and Thrives

Starting a business is exhilarating, but the statistics are sobering. Approximately **20% of small businesses fail within their first year, and about 50% fail by their fifth year** (U.S. Bureau of Labor Statistics). Understanding why is the first step to ensuring you don't become a statistic.

Top Reasons Small Businesses Fail:

1. **Running Out of Cash:** The #1 killer. Insufficient capital and poor cash flow management are fatal.
2. **No Market Need:** Creating a product or service that nobody is willing to pay for.
3. **The Wrong Team:** Incompetence, lack of experience, or internal conflict can derail even the best idea.
4. **Being Outpriced by Competition:** Failing to understand your competitive landscape and your unique value proposition.
5. **Ineffective Marketing:** Even a great product won't sell itself. A weak marketing strategy leads to no customers.

Building a Failure-Proof Business Plan

Your business plan is your strategic roadmap. It forces you to answer critical questions before you invest your time and money.

Key Questions Your Plan Must Answer:

- **Product/Market Fit:** Who is my specific customer, and why is my product/service indispensable to them?
- **Competitive Analysis:** What are my competitors doing? What makes my offering different and better?
- **Financial Projections:** What are my realistic startup costs, operating expenses, and revenue projections? What is my break-even point?
- **Contingency Planning:** What is my plan if a key supplier fails, the economy dips, or a new competitor emerges?

Operational Principles for Long-Term Success

- **Guard Your Cash Flow Religiously:** Monitor your finances daily. Cut unnecessary expenses and negotiate with suppliers. Use systems like **"Profit First"** to ensure you always prioritize profitability.
- **Make Customer Satisfaction Your Mission:** Your customers are the lifeblood of your business. Listen to their feedback, address their complaints quickly, and exceed their expectations to build loyalty.
- **Innovate and Expand Consistently:** Complacency is dangerous. Always look for new ways to grow your sales, expand your product lines, and enter new markets.

Part 3: When Things Go Wrong - A Contingency Plan for Financial Distress

Despite best efforts, sometimes businesses face insurmountable challenges. Having a contingency plan is a sign of wisdom, not weakness.

Early Warning Signs:

- Consistently struggling to pay bills on time.
- Maxing out business lines of credit.
- Dipping into personal savings to cover business costs.
- Falling behind on tax payments.

Your Action Plan if Failure Seems Imminent:

1. **Seek Professional Help Immediately:** Consult with a **certified public accountant (CPA)** and a **bankruptcy attorney**. They can provide objective advice and outline your options.
2. **Communicate with Creditors:** Be proactive. Many creditors would rather work out a modified payment plan than force you into bankruptcy.
3. **Explore Formal Options:** Understand the difference between Chapter 7 (liquidation) and Chapter 11 or 13 (reorganization). The **U.S. Courts** website (`uscourts.gov`) provides clear explanations of each.
4. **Leverage Free Business Counseling:** The **SCORE Association** (`score.org`) and the **Small Business Development Centers (SBDC)** (`americassbdc.org`) offer free, confidential mentoring and advice from experienced business professionals.

Conclusion: Resilience is the Ultimate Goal

Financial resilience, for both you and your business, is built on a foundation of knowledge, a solid plan, and the humility to seek help when needed. Avoiding bankruptcy is about proactively building that resilience through continuous education and sound management. And if the worst happens, remember that it is not an end, but a difficult reset. By addressing the root causes of financial trouble, you can emerge wiser, stronger, and better prepared for future success. Start building your knowledge and your plan today. Your financial future depends on it.

Section 3

Business Brilliance

The Mental Edge of Business Success

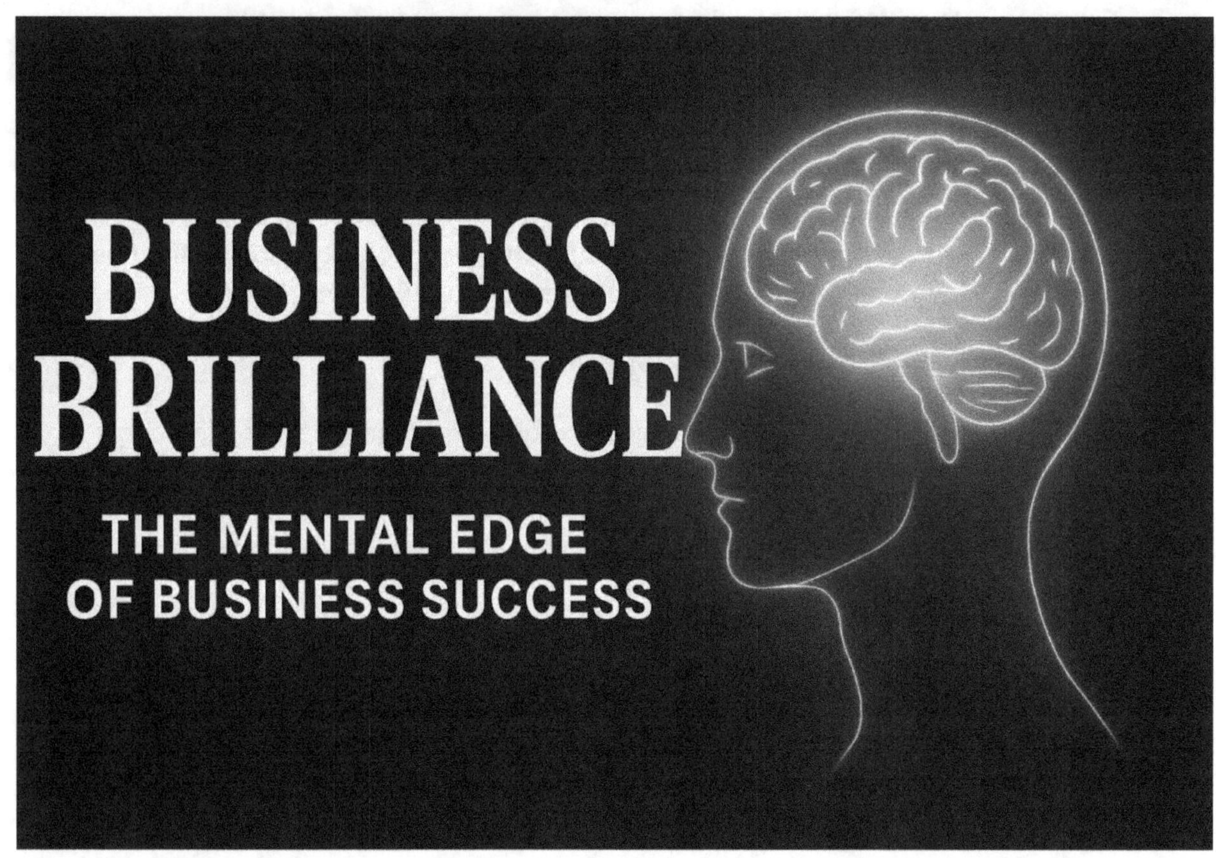

Chapter 18

The Entrepreneur's Edge

The 8 Pillars of Entrepreneurial Success

The dream of entrepreneurship is a powerful force in the American consciousness. Ask any group of people if they'd like to be their own boss, and a resounding **"yes"** would echo back. The allure of autonomy, unlimited income potential, and building something from the ground up is intoxicating. However, this dream often shadows over the gritty reality: entrepreneurship is not a fantasy escape from work; it is a demanding, all-encompassing journey that requires a specific mindset to survive and thrive.

Many aspiring founders are captivated by the vision of success but are unprepared for the sleepless nights, financial uncertainty, and relentless problem-solving that define the startup phase. True entrepreneurship is built not on a whim, but on a foundation of determination, commitment, and a strategic, living business plan.

So, how do you know if you have what it takes? Success is less about a lucky break and more about cultivating a specific way of thinking. Below, we will explore the eight essential pillars you must develop to forge a true entrepreneur's mindset and build a lasting venture.

Pillar 1: Cultivate Realistic Optimism

It's one thing to be a dreamer; it's another to be a builder. The successful entrepreneur is powered by a *realistic optimism*. They are naturally inclined to see possibilities and innovative solutions where others see obstacles. This isn't blind positivity; it's the unwavering belief that a path exists, even if it has to be carved out themselves.

- **Actionable Insight:** Keep an **"Idea tracker."** Whether it's a dedicated notebook or a digital app, consistently write down your creative and inventive business ideas. The act of writing not only preserves the idea but also encourages your brain to develop it further. Periodically review your log to see which concepts have lasting power.
- **Resource: MindTools** offers great techniques for creative thinking and innovation. (Website: https://www.mindtools.com/a1bjd74/understanding-creativity)

Pillar 2: Master the Concept of Calculated Risk-Taking

Entrepreneurship is inherently risky, but successful entrepreneurs are not gamblers. They are calculated risk-takers. They understand that risk cannot be eliminated, but it can be understood, quantified, and mitigated. Instead of asking, **"What if I fail?"** they ask, **"What is the potential loss, and is it acceptable given the potential reward?"**

Key Formulas:

- **Probability:** For independent events, you can assess chance with: `p(A and B) = p(A) * p(B)`. This helps in understanding the likelihood of multiple favorable conditions aligning.
- **Risk Assessment:** A fundamental formula is: `Risk = Probability x Impact`. This forces you to consider both the odds of a negative event happening and the severity of its consequences.
- **Resource: Harvard Business Review** frequently publishes articles on risk management and decision-making for leaders. (Website: https://hbr.org/topic/subject/risk-management)

Pillar 3: Embrace the Concept of Decisive Action Steps

An idea is worthless without execution. The chasm between a brilliant concept and a marketable product is bridged only by action. This means moving from thinking and planning to *doing*. It involves creating a minimum viable product, testing assumptions, gathering feedback, and iterating quickly. Perfection is the enemy of progress.

- **Actionable Insight:** Break down your grand vision into the smallest possible action step. What can you do *today* to move your idea forward? It could be as simple as sketching a prototype, registering a domain name, or having a conversation with a potential customer.

Pillar 4: Drive Your Vision with Relentless Improvement

Entrepreneurs see the world through a lens of **"how can this be better?"** They are naturally dissatisfied with the status quo. This isn't about criticism; it's about opportunity. By critically analyzing competitors' products or services, you can identify gaps, pain points, and unmet customer needs that your venture can address.

- **Actionable Insight:** Conduct a **"Competitive Analysis."** List your top three competitors and identify three things they do well and three areas where they fall short. Your competitive advantage lies in those shortcomings.

Pillar 5: Thrive on Problem-Solving

Challenges are not roadblocks for the entrepreneurial mind; they are the curriculum. The journey of building a business is a continuous series of problems to be solved, from supply chain hiccups to marketing misfires. If you are someone who feels energized by a tough puzzle and possesses the resilience to think your way through difficult scenarios, you have a key entrepreneurial trait.

- **Resource: Farnam Street Blog** (https://fs.blog) is dedicated to mastering the best of what other people have already figured out, providing mental models for better thinking and problem-solving.

Pillar 6: Develop Opportunity Radar

Successful entrepreneurs have a tuned **"Opportunity Radar."** They are constantly scanning their environment for new trends, emerging technologies, and shifting consumer behaviors that signal a money-making opportunity. This isn't about being opportunistic in a negative sense; it's about being alert and agile enough to pivot or expand when the right chance appears.

- **Actionable Insight:** Dedicate 30 minutes each week to reading industry reports, trend forecasts, or tech news. Sites like **TrendWatching** (https://www.trendwatching.com) or **Exploding Topics** (https://explodingtopics.com) can help sharpen your radar.

Pillar 7: Practice Strategic Focus Habits

An entrepreneur's mind is always at work, but not on trivialities. They understand that their most valuable asset is their time and mental energy. Therefore, they practice strategic focus, delegating or automating minor tasks to concentrate on high-impact activities that drive the business forward, the vision, strategy, and key relationships.

- **Actionable Insight:** Audit your weekly tasks. Identify which activities are "low-value/high-time" and seek solutions to outsource, automate, or eliminate them. This frees up your focus for the work that only you can do.

Pillar 8: Reject the Tyranny of Becoming "Average"

For the true entrepreneur, the fear of being average is a more powerful motivator than the fear of failure. They are driven by an intrinsic desire to be exceptional, to create a legacy, and to be at the top of their field. This pillar is about holding yourself to a higher standard in everything from product quality to customer service, refusing to settle for mediocrity.

- **Actionable Insight:** Define what **"exceptional"** means for your business. Is it 99.9% product reliability? Is it 24/7 customer support? Write down your standard of excellence and make it the non-negotiable core of your company culture.

Your Journey Begins Now

Forging this founder's mindset is the first and most critical startup you will ever build. The path of entrepreneurship is challenging demanding long hours, unwavering discipline, and a resilient spirit. However, by consciously developing these eight pillars, you move from being a dreamer to a doer. You transform the abstract desire for success into a concrete capacity for it.

Arm yourself with this mindset, pair it with a solid business plan, and apply your knowledge with relentless action. The road to success is built one intentional, strategic step at a time. Are you ready to begin?

Chapter 19

The Modern Business Blueprint

7 Foundational Pillars for Building a Thriving Business

While every successful enterprise begins with a great idea, its longevity is built on a much stronger foundation. Lasting success requires a powerful combination of visionary leadership, a dynamic team, and a strategic plan that anticipates the future. If you look at the giants of industry, the Fortune 500 companies, you'll see they all share a common DNA:

- **Visionary Leadership:** A leader who articulates a clear and compelling vision for the future.
- **Dynamic Management:** A team capable of executing that vision and adapting to new challenges.
- **Exceptional Products/Services:** Offerings that genuinely resonate with and delight their customers.
- **A Living Business Plan:** A strategic roadmap that guides growth and is regularly updated to reflect a changing market.

These principles are universal, but applying them in today's digital economy requires a fresh approach. Here are the seven golden rules to guide any business owner toward sustainable success.

The 7 Pillars of Modern Business Success

1. Cultivate a Culture of "Out-of-the-Box" Thinking

In the digital age, traditional problem-solving often falls short. The most complex challenges, from engaging the millennial market to navigating global supply chains, demand creative, non-linear solutions. This means encouraging your team to question established norms and explore radical ideas.

- **In Practice:** Look to pioneers like Steve Jobs, who reimagined the phone as a lifestyle hub, or Elon Musk, who challenged the entire automotive and aerospace industries. Their success wasn't just about better technology; it was about a fundamentally different perspective. Foster this by hosting regular, no-holds-barred brainstorming sessions where **"bad ideas"** are welcomed as stepping stones to great ones.
- **Resource to Explore: IDEO**, a leading design and innovation consulting firm, is famous for its human-centered design thinking process. Their website (**https://www.ideo.com**)

and their founder Tim Brown's book, *Change by Design*, are excellent resources for learning how to build creativity into your organization's DNA.

2. Be First to the Future: Win by Seeing What Others Don't

In business, the **"finish line"** is often an untapped market or an unmet customer need. The goal is to identify these opportunities before your competitors do. This requires foresight, the ability to connect trends and see where the industry is heading.

- **In Practice:** Don't just ask what your customers want now; anticipate what they will need tomorrow. Amazon didn't just sell books online; it foresaw a future where everything could be delivered, leading to its world-class logistics and AWS cloud division. Continuously scan the horizon for technological shifts, demographic changes, and **"gaps in the wall"** that your business is uniquely positioned to fill.
- **Resource to Explore:** https://www.trendwatching.com provides free insights and reports on consumer trends and innovation from around the world. Use their resources to spot emerging behaviors that could signal your next big opportunity.

3. Leverage Diversity as Your Strategic Advantage

Diversity is far more than a metric; it's a critical driver of innovation. A team with varied backgrounds, cultures, genders, and experiences brings a wider range of perspectives to the table. This diversity is your best defense against groupthink and a powerful tool for problem-solving.

- **In Practice:** A homogenous team will likely approach a problem in a homogenous way. A diverse team will challenge assumptions, reveal cultural blind spots, and help you understand a global customer base more deeply. Actively seek out and create an inclusive environment for these diverse voices, and then *listen to them.*
- **Resource to Explore: Diversity** (https://greatergood.berkeley.edu/topic/diversity/definition) offers research, news, and best practices on diversity and inclusion in the corporate world. Their rankings and articles can provide a roadmap for building a more effective and innovative organization.

4. Lead with Generosity: The Virtuous Cycle of Giving

Success creates an opportunity for reciprocity. Generosity builds immense goodwill, strengthens your brand, and fosters loyalty, both internally with your team and externally with your customers. People are drawn to companies that demonstrate authentic care and contribute to their community.

- **In Practice:** This goes beyond charitable donations. It can mean offering exceptional customer service that goes the extra mile, sharing profits with employees through bonuses or stock options, or allowing company time for volunteer work. Companies like

Patagonia, with its commitment to environmental causes, have built fiercely loyal communities around their generous and authentic ethos.

- **Resource to Explore: B Lab (https://www.bcorporation.net/en-us)** certifies companies that meet high standards of social and environmental performance. Exploring the B Corp directory can provide inspiration for how to integrate generosity and social responsibility into your business model.

5. Architect the Perfect Team: It's About Fit, Not Just Credentials

A large corporation is a complex machine with many interdependent parts. Your role as a leader is to be an architect, carefully placing the right people in the right roles. Look beyond impressive resumes and prestigious schools to find individuals whose skills, values, and collaborative spirit align with your company's mission.

- **In Practice:** A brilliant coder might be a terrible team lead. A sales superstar might undermine company culture. Hire for complementary skills and cultural add, not just cultural fit. Ensure every team member understands how their role contributes to the overarching vision, empowering them to use their unique talents to move the company forward.
- **Resource to Explore:** The book *Who: The A Method for Hiring* by Geoff Smart and Randy Street provides a disciplined framework for making successful hiring decisions, helping you avoid common pitfalls and find **"A Players."**

6. Invest in Your People: Your Most Appreciating Asset

Once you have the right team, your most important job is to invest in their growth. This includes formal training and professional development, but also creating a supportive environment where they feel valued and heard. When you invest in your people, you are investing in the future capability of your company.

- **In Practice:** Look for and nurture key qualities like integrity, perseverance, and a collaborative spirit. Provide mentorship programs, sponsor skills courses, and create clear paths for career advancement. An employee who feels the company is invested in their success will reciprocate with greater loyalty, innovation, and productivity.
- **Resource to Explore:** Platforms like **LinkedIn Learning** and **Coursera** offer thousands of affordable courses to help upskill your team in everything from software development to soft skills, demonstrating your commitment to their growth.

7. Become Obsessed with Customer Value

Your customers are the lifeblood of your business. This isn't a cliché; it's a fundamental truth. A customer-centric business doesn't just sell *to* people; it solves problems *for* them. Every decision, from product development to marketing, should be made with the customer's experience and perceived value in mind.

- **In Practice:** Actively gather and act on customer feedback. Use surveys, social media listening, and direct interviews. Tailor your offerings to their evolving needs. Companies like Apple and Zappos command premium prices and fierce loyalty because they have built their entire operation around delivering an exceptional customer experience.
- **Resource to Explore: SurveyMonkey** or **Typeform** are excellent tools for creating and distributing customer satisfaction (CSAT) and Net Promoter Score (NPS) surveys to gather actionable feedback directly from your audience.

Conclusion: Your Blueprint for Action

Success in the modern business landscape is not accidental. It is built deliberately upon these seven pillars. By fostering innovation, anticipating the future, embracing diversity, leading with generosity, building a world-class team, investing relentlessly in your people, and maintaining an unwavering focus on customer value, you create an organization built not just to compete, but to lead. Review this blueprint, implement these ideas with intention, and watch as you build a business that is both profitable and enduring.

Chapter 20

The Wealth Builder's Blueprint

8 Asset Classes the Rich Acquire

(That The Poor Overspend On)

Introduction: The Fundamental Mindset Shift

Before we can understand the spending habits of the wealthy, we must first master a fundamental financial concept: the difference between an asset and a liability. This is the foundational principle that separates wealth builders from those who struggle financially.

- **An Asset** is anything that puts money *into* your pocket. It generates income, appreciates in value, or both, thereby increasing your net worth over time. Think of assets as your loyal employees, working for you 24/7.
- **A Liability** is anything that takes money *out* of your pocket. It costs you money to own, maintain, or operate, thereby draining your wealth. These are the financial burdens that keep you on the treadmill.

Many in the working class find themselves in a cycle of high expenses and debt, constantly trading their time for money on a job. To break free, the focus must shift from simply earning a higher salary to **acquiring more income-generating assets** while simultaneously **minimizing costly liabilities.**

Here are the eight powerful asset classes the wealthy consistently invest in.

1. Revenue-Generating Businesses: The Engine of Wealth

For the wealthy, a job is not the primary source of income; it's a starting point or a temporary vehicle. Their top priority is owning businesses that generate profits independently of their direct labor.

Why it Works: A well-structured business systemizes income. It can run with a team, generate cash flow, and be scaled or sold. This is the ultimate form of financial leverage, using a system to create wealth.

Getting Started: You don't have to start from scratch.

- **Franchises:** Buy into a proven business model.

  `FranchiseGator.com` - Explore franchises with various investment levels.
  https://www.franchisegator.com

  `FranchiseDirect.com` - Find opportunities for under $25,000.
  https://www.franchisedirect.com

- **Acquisition:** Purchase an existing, profitable business.

  `BizBuySell.com` - The largest marketplace to buy an established business.
  https://www.bizbuysell.com

  `WebsiteClosers.com` & `WoodbridgeGrp.com` - Brokerages specializing in the sale of companies. https://woodbridgegrp.com

2. Income-Producing Real Estate: The Tangible Cash Flow

The wealthy don't just own a home; they own properties that pay them. While their primary residence is often a liability (due to mortgages, taxes, and upkeep), their investment properties are assets designed for cash flow and appreciation.

Why it Works: Real estate provides multiple wealth-building avenues: monthly rental income (cash flow), property value appreciation over time, and significant tax advantages. Commercial and multi-unit residential properties magnify these benefits.

Getting Started: You no longer need millions to invest in large-scale real estate.

- **Real Estate Crowdfunding:** Pool your money with other investors.

  `Fundrise.com` - Allows you to invest in private real estate portfolios.
  https://fundrise.com

  `DiversyFund.com` - Focuses on growth-focused real estate investments.
  https://diversyfund.com

3. Paper Assets: The Liquid Wealth Machine

"Paper assets" like stocks, bonds, ETFs (Exchange-Traded Funds), and mutual funds are core components of any wealthy individual's portfolio due to their high liquidity and growth potential.

Why it Works: These assets represent ownership in thousands of companies and funds. They can be bought and sold instantly on public exchanges, providing high liquidity. The power of compounding returns and dividend reinvestment over decades is unparalleled.

Getting Started: The barriers to entry are lower than ever.

- **Commission-Free Brokerages:**

  `Fidelity.com` or Vanguard.com - Industry giants known for low-cost index funds. **https://www.fidelity.com , https://investor.vanguard.com**

  `M1Finance.com` - Allows for automated, customizable investing **"pies."** **https://m1.com**

- **Robo-Advisors & Micro-Investing:**

  `Betterment.com` - Provides automated, goal-based investing. **https://www.betterment.com**

  `Acorns.com` - Automatically invests your **"spare change."** **https://www.acorns.com**

4. Fine Art & Collectibles: The Store of Value

Beyond aesthetics, fine art, antiques, and rare collectibles are a sophisticated asset class. The wealthy use them to preserve and grow capital in a tangible form that often has a low correlation to the stock market.

Why it Works: Rare pieces by renowned artists or from specific eras can appreciate significantly. This asset class acts as a **"store of value"** and a hedge against inflation.

Getting Started: Research is key.

- **Auction Houses & Galleries:**

  `Artsy.net` - A massive online platform for discovering and collecting art. **https://www.artsy.net**

  `Sothebys.com` & `Christies.com` - World-renowned auction houses for high-end art and antiques. **https://www.christies.com , https://www.sothebys.com/en**

5. Classic & Exotic Automobiles: The Rolling Assets

While a new car is a rapidly depreciating liability, a curated collection of classic or exotic cars can be a powerful appreciating asset.

Why it Works: Scarcity and historical significance drive up the value of certain vehicles. The wealthy treat them as a passion investment that can be liquidated for a profit.

Getting Started: The market is highly specialized.

- **Major Auction Houses:**

  `Barrett-Jackson.com` & `Mecum.com` - The premier names in collector car auctions. **https://www.barrett-jackson.com** , **https://www.mecum.com**

  `BringATrailer.com` - A popular online auction platform for enthusiast cars. **https://bringatrailer.com**

6. Intellectual Property: The Invisible Goldmine

Intellectual Property (IP), patents, trademarks, and copyrights, is the ownership of ideas. The wealthy understand that controlling a unique process, brand, or creation can generate massive, passive income through licensing.

Why it Works: A single patent for a useful invention or a popular character trademark can earn royalties for decades without any further active work from the owner.

Getting Started: Protecting your ideas is the first step.

- **The U.S. Patent and Trademark Office** - The official government site to file for patents and trademarks. **https://www.uspto.gov**
- **Legal Platforms:**

  `UpCounsel.com` - Connect with attorneys who specialize in IP law. https://www.upcounsel.com

7. Hard Assets & Precious Metals: The Ultimate Safety Net

Gold, silver, and other precious metals have been a trusted store of wealth for millennia. The wealthy use them as a portfolio diversifier and a hedge against economic uncertainty and currency devaluation.

Why it Works: Precious metals are a physical store of value that isn't tied to any government or company. They tend to hold their value during times of geopolitical or financial instability.

Getting Started: Focus on reputable dealers.

- **Bullion Dealers:**

  `JM Bullion (JMBullion.com)` & `SD Bullion (SDBullion.com)` - Well-regarded online dealers for gold and silver coins and bars. **https://www.jmbullion.com** , **https://sdbullion.com**

The Bonus Asset Class: Your Personal Brand

Even if you start with zero capital, this asset class is available to everyone. It's called **Personal Branding**.

What it Is: Your personal brand is the value you offer to a specific audience. It's the reputation and influence you build by sharing your knowledge, skills, and personality. Think of influencers, authors, speakers, and experts who have built a loyal following.

Why it Works: In the digital age, a strong personal brand is a powerful business asset. It allows you to:

- Monetize your audience through courses, sponsorships, and product sales.
- Command higher fees for your services or speaking engagements.
- Launch successful products with a built-in customer base.

How to Build It: This asset requires investment in *yourself*, in your knowledge and your ability to communicate value. It's built consistently over time on platforms like YouTube, LinkedIn, podcasts, and newsletters by solving problems for and adding value to your target audience.

Conclusion: Your Path Forward

Understanding the distinction between assets and liabilities is the first step. The next is to act. Your financial future will be determined not by your salary, but by the quality and quantity of the assets you acquire.

Review these eight asset classes. Identify one or two that resonate with you and begin your research. Start building your personal brand today, as it requires no capital, only commitment. By shifting your focus from consumption to acquisition, you are not just changing your spending habits, you are adopting the **Wealth Builder's Blueprint.**

Chapter 21

The Creator of Abundance

Building a Millionaire Mindset from the Ground Up

Introduction

What separates the visionary entrepreneur from the dreamer? It isn't just a stroke of luck or a revolutionary idea. The world's most successful business leaders operate like master architects. They don't just have a blueprint for a single house; they understand the principles of building entire cities. They are experts at designing resilient structures (their businesses), sourcing the finest materials (their teams), and adapting their plans to withstand any storm (market challenges).

If you are new to the entrepreneurial journey, the first step is to adopt this architectural mindset. The primary question they ask isn't just **"Will this make money?"** but a more profound one: **"How can I build something that is meaningfully better, that serves a need, and that stands the test of time?"** Let's deconstruct the core habits that form the foundation of this millionaire mindset, habits you can start building today.

The 10 Cornerstone Habits for Extraordinary Success

1. Cultivate a Compelling Vision

Your vision is the master blueprint for your venture. It's a vivid, compelling picture of the future you are committed to creating. A well-defined vision acts as your guide. When challenges arise, and they will, a clear vision provides clarity and purpose, allowing you to navigate obstacles without losing your way. You're not just solving a problem; you're removing a barrier on the path to your defined destination.

- **Helpful Resource:** The **Simon Sinek "Start With Why**" framework is a powerful tool for clarifying your vision. Explore his TED Talk and books to understand how to communicate your vision inspire others.

2. Reframe and Conquer Challenges

Setbacks are not roadblocks; they are an integral part of the construction process. The key differentiator between success and failure is your response to adversity. While some fall into self-pity or destructive coping mechanisms, the successful individual sees a challenge as a complex equation waiting to be solved. The habit is to:

- **Acknowledge** The problem clearly and without panic.
- **Analyze** The root cause.
- **Architect** Multiple potential solutions.
  When you're stuck, consult a trusted mentor, a fellow **"Architect"** who can offer a fresh perspective and help you see a solution you may have missed.

3. Execute with Strategic Action

A vision without action remains a fantasy. The habit of taking *strategic* action is what bridges the gap between idea and reality. This requires analytical thinking and meticulous planning. Before breaking ground, you must research, sequence your steps, and allocate resources. If you are uncertain about the next right move, don't guess, consult an expert. An hour with a seasoned professional can save you months of misdirected effort.

- **Helpful Resource: https://www.score.org** offers free mentorship from retired business executives. It's an invaluable resource for vetting your action plans.

4. Master the Art of Talent Leverage

No architect builds a skyscraper alone. The habit of leveraging talent is about recognizing that your success is multiplied through the skills of others. Your role is to be the chief identifier of talent, finding the best engineers, designers, and project managers for your dream. Once you have them, your job is to empower them. Pay them well, provide them with top-tier tools, and give them the autonomy to excel in their areas of genius. This allows you to focus on the overall vision and growth.

5. Take Intelligent, Calculated Risks

Life is inherently risky. The goal is not to avoid risk, but to manage it intelligently. Millionaires take *calculated* risks. This means rigorously assessing the potential upside versus the potential downside. You weigh the pros and cons, conduct market research, and make informed decisions. You never bet the entire company on a hunch. This disciplined approach allows you to seize significant opportunities without jeopardizing your foundation.

6. Lead with Authentic Influence

Leadership is not a title; it's a behavior. Effective leadership begins with leading your own life with integrity and purpose. Great leaders are honest communicators, decisive, empathetic, and inspirational. They set the standard for the entire organization and are dedicated to developing the leadership potential in others. They don't just manage tasks; they manage energy and culture, creating an environment where people are motivated to contribute their best work.

- **Helpful Resource: Dale Carnegie's** classic book, *How to Win Friends and Influence People*, remains a masterclass in the human principles of leadership.

7. Develop a Genuine Interest in People

Business is a human enterprise. The habit of being a **"People Person"** is about cultivating authentic connections. It means being approachable, showing genuine curiosity about others, and demonstrating that you care. As the saying goes, **"People don't care what you know until**

they know how much you care." When your team and clients feel valued as individuals, their loyalty and commitment to your shared vision deepen exponentially.

8. Think and Plan on a Grand Scale

Your brain uses the same energy to dream small as it does to dream big. So, why think small? The habit of thinking big involves stretching your vision across multiple timelines. Visualize where you want your business to be in one year, five years, and even two decades. This long-range perspective forces you to consider industry trends, innovation, and scalability, ensuring your business remains relevant and dominant far into the future.

9. Embrace the Power of Delegation

Delegation is the practical application of talent leverage. It is the conscious habit of entrusting tasks to the people best equipped to handle them. This frees you, the visionary, to operate at your highest level of impact. Effective delegation isn't abdication; it's empowerment supported by mentorship, training, and clear communication. It's about building a team that doesn't just work *for* you, but works *with* you to achieve the common vision.

- **Helpful Resource:** The **Eisenhower Decision Matrix** is a simple tool to help you categorize tasks by urgency and importance, making it clear what you should delegate.

10. Build an Irresistible Personal Brand

In today's world, you are your brand. Your brand is the promise of the value you deliver. It's the reputation that precedes you and the memory that lingers after you're gone. Building a powerful brand requires consistency, authenticity, and a relentless commitment to quality. Your customers should not only desire your product but also trust and respect the name behind it. This takes time and investment, but a strong brand becomes your most valuable asset, attracting opportunities and customers on autopilot.

- **Helpful Resource: Personal Branding Blog by Dan Schawbel** offers a wealth of articles and insights on how to build and maintain a powerful personal brand.

Conclusion: You Are the Architect of Your Future

We have just explored the ten cornerstone habits that form the mindset of a millionaire. These are not secret tricks, but fundamental principles of building something significant from the ground up. You don't need a massive inheritance or a lucky break; you need the discipline to lay one brick perfectly after another.

By internalizing and acting on these habits, by becoming the architect of your own abundance, you are not just chasing success. You are engineering it. The blueprint is in your hands. Now, it's time to build.

Chapter 22

The Art of Influence

Mastering Persuasion and the Principle of Reciprocity

Introduction: More Than Just Getting Your Way

Persuasion is not about manipulation or coercion; it is the art of ethically guiding someone toward a shared understanding or a mutually beneficial action. It is the invisible force behind successful leadership, thriving businesses, and healthy relationships. The dictionary defines **persuasion** as **"the process aimed at changing a person's (or a group's) attitude or behavior."** This is achieved through communication, spoken, written, or a blend of both.

But what does being persuasive mean to you? For many, it's the ability to inspire, to build consensus, and to lead with vision. True persuasion is an exercise in trust and connection.

The Foundation: Integrity, Leadership, and Communication

Before you can persuade anyone of anything, you must first have their full attention. To keep it, you must build a foundation of trust. A persuader must operate with integrity and demonstrate genuine leadership skills. People are far more likely to be convinced by someone they respect and believe in.

This is especially true in positions of formal authority. When you are a leader, the power of persuasion can come more easily, but it also carries greater responsibility. Your role is to communicate your vision with clarity and guide your team toward success. However, this trust is fragile. The quickest way to shatter your influence is to use it to convince people to do something that brings them harm. Once lost, trust is incredibly difficult to regain.

Persuasion in the Wild: A Constant in Our Lives

Look around, and you will see persuasion at work everywhere:

- **Politicians** work to persuade the public they are the right choice for the job.
- **Corporations** spend billions on marketing, persuading us that their product is superior to a competitor's.
- **World leaders and celebrities** leverage their platforms to persuade us to believe in their ideas and causes.
- **Our parents** used persuasion throughout our childhoods to guide our behavior, often toward outcomes that were for our own good, though sometimes, unfortunately, toward paths that were not.

Recognizing these daily attempts to influence us is the first step in becoming a more conscious consumer of information and a more ethical influencer ourselves.

The Golden Rule of Influence: The Principle of Reciprocity

While integrity and communication are the bedrock, specific psychological principles make persuasion more effective. One of the most powerful is **Reciprocity**.

What is Reciprocity?

The dictionary defines **reciprocity** as **"the practice of exchanging things with others for mutual benefit."** In social psychology, it is a fundamental rule: we are hardwired to feel obligated to repay what others have given us. This isn't about cold calculation; it's a deep-seated social norm that helps build cooperative relationships.

How Reciprocity Works in Practice:

- **In the Workplace:** If a colleague helps you meet a tight deadline, you are naturally more inclined to help them on a future project.
- **In Social Settings:** If you buy a friend lunch unexpectedly, they will likely feel a strong desire to pay for the next meal.
- **In Business:** A company that provides a free, high-value sample or a helpful consultancy report is leveraging reciprocity. The client feels a subconscious pull to reciprocate, often by making a purchase.

A closely related concept is **"Paying It Forward,"** where a recipient of a good deed repays it to another person instead of the original benefactor, creating a chain of generosity.

The Key to Effective Reciprocity: The gesture must be perceived as genuine, useful, and provided without strings attached. It should be a gift, not an immediate trade. When done correctly, the return on that goodwill often comes back twofold.

A Note on the "Takers":
Reciprocity is a powerful rule, but it is not absolute. It may not work on profoundly selfish individuals, those who consistently prioritize their own needs without regard for others. While it's important to recognize this, building a strategy around the exception is a mistake. The principle holds true for the vast majority of people. If you find yourself consistently surrounded by **"takers,"** the best course is to re-evaluate your circle rather than abandon a proven principle of human connection.

Becoming a Master Influencer

Mastering persuasion is a journey. Once you have securely established yourself as a person of integrity, a clear communicator, and a genuine leader, influencing others becomes a natural extension of your relationships. People will be more open to your ideas because they trust your intentions.

In Conclusion: Your Path Forward

To become a truly persuasive person, focus on these core areas:

- **Cultivate Unshakable Integrity.** Be trustworthy and ethical in all your dealings.
- **Hone Your Communication.** Learn to articulate your ideas with clarity and passion.
- **Practice Ethical Influence.** Use principles like reciprocity not as tricks, but as ways to build genuine goodwill.

Be the first to extend help, offer support, and show kindness without any immediate expectation of return. Do it because it is the right thing to do. The profound, underlying psychology is that the person on the receiving end will feel a natural and positive obligation to reciprocate in the future. In the art of persuasion, generosity is not an expense; it is an investment in your relationships and your influence.

Resources for Deeper Learning

To further your understanding of persuasion and influence, explore these reputable resources:

Books:

- ***Influence: The Psychology of Persuasion* by Dr. Robert Cialdini.** This is the seminal work on the subject, where Dr. Cialdini outlines his six key principles of influence, including Reciprocity. It is essential reading.
- ***Pre-Suasion: A Revolutionary Way to Influence and Persuade* by Dr. Robert Cialdini.** A follow-up that explores how to set the stage for persuasion before you even make a request.

Websites and Organizations:

- **The Society for Personality and Social Psychology (SPSP):** `https://spsp.org` A great resource for accessing the latest research in social psychology, including studies on persuasion and pro-social behavior.
- **Farnam Street Blog (fs.blog):** `https://fs.blog` This site is dedicated to mastering the best of what other people have already figured out. It frequently features excellent articles on mental models, cognitive biases, and the principles of influence, often breaking down Cialdini's work.

Concept Explained:

- **"Paying It Forward" Foundation:** `https://lead.osu.edu/community-engagement/pay-it-forward` Learn more about the global movement inspired by this concept of reciprocal generosity.

Chapter 23

The Art of The Deal (Negotiation)

A Strategic Guide to Closing Deals

What is Negotiation, Really?

The dictionary defines negotiation as **"a method by which people settle differences"** or **"a process by which a compromise or agreement is reached while avoiding argument and dispute."**

While this definition provides a basic framework, it misses the core of what makes business negotiation so powerful. In the world of business, negotiation is not about winning a battle; it's a strategic dance aimed at creating value and building lasting partnerships. It's the art of finding a solution that feels like a victory for all parties involved, ensuring that the deal closed today is the foundation for the deal you'll make tomorrow.

Mastering this art is not an innate talent but a learnable skill. By understanding a structured process and key tactics, you can approach every discussion with confidence and dramatically increase your success rate.

The 3-Step Strategic Negotiation Process

Move beyond haggling and embrace a process designed for optimal outcomes.

Step 1: Diagnose the Landscape – (See Through Their Eyes)

Before you even state your position, your most critical task is to understand theirs. The most successful negotiators are, first and foremost, exceptional listeners and empathizers.

- **Go Beyond the Price Tag:** Ask yourself: What are their underlying interests? Are they under pressure to meet a quarterly goal? Is this deal more about prestige, market share, or solving a specific operational headache? What does **"value'** truly mean to them?
- **The Power of Perspective:** By genuinely putting yourself in their shoes, you can frame your proposals in a way that resonates with their needs. This isn't about manipulation; it's about alignment. When you can articulate the value of your proposal ***from their perspective,*** you transform the conversation from a transactional debate into a collaborative problem-solving session. This builds trust and lays the groundwork for a long-term relationship, not just a one-time transaction.

Step 2: Anchor the Outcome – (Ask for More Than You Need)

A classic and powerful strategy, this step is about setting the stage in your favor.

- **Know Your Walk-Away Point:** Before negotiations begin, you must define your limits. What is your **BATNA** (Best Alternative To a Negotiated Agreement)? Knowing your BATNA, your best option if the deal falls through, gives you the power to walk away confidently. Alongside this, set your **reservation point** (the absolute minimum you will accept) and your **target point** (your ambitious but realistic goal).
- **The Anchoring Effect:** By starting with an ambitious but justifiable opening offer (e.g., asking for $8,000 when your target is $5,000), you set a psychological **"anchor."** This anchor becomes the reference point for the entire discussion. Even when you negotiate **"down"** to your actual target, the other party often feels they have **"won"** by moving you from your initial number. This not only helps you hit your target but can often secure a bonus above it.

Step 3: Protect the Relationship – Preserve Your Role as a Partner

Not every negotiation will end in a handshake. How you handle a breakdown is just as important as how you handle a success.

- **The "Higher Authority" Gambit:** If a deal is stalling or turning negative, avoid taking personal blame. A highly effective method is to leverage a absent **"higher authority."** You can position yourself as an advocate for the deal while explaining that final approval lies with a committee, your boss, or your partners.
- **How to Execute It:** Phrase it collaboratively: **"I love the direction this is heading, and I'm fully on board. To get this across the finish line, I'll need to present these final terms to my finance team for their sign-off. Let me see if I can advocate for this with them."** This tactic does three things: it gives you time to think, it allows you to potentially re-negotiate **("My team is pushing back on X, is there any way we can Y?"),** and, most importantly, it shields the personal relationship you've built. The disappointment is directed at a faceless **"entity,"** not you, keeping the door open for future business.

In Closing: The Negotiator's Mindset

Successful negotiation is a blend of preparation, psychology, and ethics. Always enter a negotiation having diagnosed the other party's deeper interests. Use strategic anchors to create a favorable bargaining range. And finally, conduct yourself in a way that preserves relationships, using tactics like the higher authority to avoid being the **"bad guy."** By doing so, you ensure that regardless of the outcome of a single deal, your reputation as a fair, strategic, and trustworthy partner remains intact.

Additional Resources to Sharpen Your Skills

To continue your development, explore these world-renowned concepts and resources:

- **Getting to Yes: Negotiating Agreement Without Giving In** by Roger Fisher and William Ury. This book introduces the foundational concepts of **principled negotiation**, focusing on interests, not positions.
- **Concept: BATNA (Best Alternative To a Negotiated Agreement):** Popularized by **"Getting to Yes,"** understanding your BATNA is the single most important source of your negotiating power.
- **Concept: Anchoring:** A cognitive bias where the first number put on the table sets a mental benchmark for the rest of the discussion.

Helpful Websites:

1. **Program on Negotiation at Harvard Law School:** Their website (**https://www.pon.harvard.edu**) is a treasure trove of free articles, blog posts, and research on every aspect of negotiation, from daily life to high-stakes corporate deals.
2. **Negotiation Experts:** Websites like **https://www.negotiations.com** offer tips, courses, and articles that break down complex strategies into actionable advice.
3. **LinkedIn Learning:** Platforms like LinkedIn Learning (**https://www.linkedin.com/learning** **)** host numerous high-quality courses on negotiation skills taught by industry experts, allowing you to learn at your own pace.

Chapter 24

The Connector's Advantage

Building Wealth Through Relationships

Introduction: Beyond "What You Know"

We've all heard the adage, **"It's not what you know, but who you know."** While this holds a core of truth, it's an incomplete picture. In today's world, the true power of networking isn't just about *who* you know, it's about **who knows you, trusts you, and is willing to advocate for you.** When cultivated with intention and integrity, your network becomes a living ecosystem of mutual support, opening doors to unparalleled business opportunities, pivotal client relationships, and lifelong mentorships.

This chapter will guide you in shifting your mindset from **"Networking"** as a transactional task to **"connecting"** as a strategic, value-driven investment in your future.

The Core Principle: Give First, Receive Later

The most successful networkers operate on a simple but powerful principle: **be a value-first investor in your relationships.**

Think of your network not as a contact list, but as a portfolio of long-term investments. You wouldn't expect to deposit one dollar today and withdraw a million tomorrow. Similarly, you must first invest your time, knowledge, and genuine support into a relationship. You build social capital, the currency of trust and goodwill. Only after this account has matured can you ethically and effectively draw upon its wealth.

This means that when you want to form a new connection, your first question should not be, **"What can this person do for me?"** but rather, **"How can I add value to this person's life or business?"** Demonstrate the benefits you bring to the table. Establish a personable, trusting foundation first. The cultivation of favors and resources comes later, naturally, as a byproduct of a genuine connection.

The Pillars of Powerful Connections

To build a network that lasts, focus on these three foundational pillars:

1. Trust: The Non-Negotiable Foundation

Trust is the bedrock of every meaningful professional relationship. It's built on a simple, yet challenging, concept: **personal integrity.** This means you must consistently say what you mean and do exactly what you say. When people know they can rely on your word, your value in their eyes increases exponentially. Trust transforms a casual contact into a committed ally. Without it, your network is fragile; with it, your network becomes an unshakable asset.

2. Genuine Interest: The Magnetic Force

People have an innate ability to sense when someone is genuinely interested in them. As the saying goes, **"People don't care what you know until they know how much you care."**

To practice this:

- **Listen Actively:** Go beyond small talk. Take time to understand a person's goals, challenges, interests, and even their fears.
- **Find Ways to Add Value:** Once you understand their needs, connect them with a resource, share a relevant article, or offer a piece of helpful advice.
- **Be Authentic:** Avoid being a pushover or putting on a facade. Let your curiosity and care come naturally. People are drawn to authenticity and can quickly detect deception.

3. Mentorship: The Accelerator for Growth

One of the most powerful aspects of networking is finding guidance. Actively seek out and connect with like-minded individuals who are on a similar path, as well as those who are a few steps ahead.

- **Find a Mentor:** Look for someone whose career or personal development you admire. A good mentor can offer invaluable advice, open doors, and help you avoid common pitfalls.
- **Join a Mastermind:** Partner with a group of peers who share similar goals. This creates a powerful environment for exchanging ideas, holding each other accountable, and reaching your maximum potential together.

Networking in the Digital Age

In our hyper-connected world, your online presence is an integral part of your networking strategy. It's no longer separate from **"real life."** Employers, clients, and partners routinely look at social profiles to gauge a prospect's professionalism, interests, and character.

Your digital footprint is your modern-day handshake. It's crucial to be a master at cultivating positive and professional connections online, ensuring your virtual persona aligns with the trustworthy, value-driven individual you are in person.

Actionable Resources to Build Your Network

To put these principles into practice, here are some valuable websites and platforms:

- **For Professional Connections:**

  LinkedIn: The undisputed leader for professional networking. Optimize your profile, share insightful content, and engage meaningfully in industry groups. **https://www.linkedin.com**

- **For Finding Local Events & Meetups:**

  Meetup: Find local groups and events related to your industry, hobbies, or professional interests. **https://www.meetup.com**

  Eventbrite: A great platform to discover workshops, seminars, and networking mixers in your city. **https://www.eventbrite.com**

- **For Industry-Specific Insights & Connections:**

  Clubhouse: An audio-based social app where you can join "rooms" and listen to or participate in conversations on thousands of topics. It's excellent for virtual networking and learning.

  Professional Associations: Almost every industry has one (e.g., American Marketing Association, Project Management Institute). Joining provides access to exclusive events, directories, and publications.

Conclusion: Your Network is Your Net Worth

The power of networking with people who share your goals, dreams, and passions is immeasurable. It is the force that turns individual effort into collective achievement. By focusing on giving value first, building unwavering trust, and showing genuine care, you will transform your network from a list of contacts into a powerful community, a community that will not only propel your career but also enrich your personal journey. Start building your connector's advantage today.

Chapter 25

The Resilient Enterprise

Navigating Crisis and Capitalizing on Post-Pandemic Growth

Introduction: The New Business Reality

The global shutdown of 2020 wasn't just a temporary disruption; it was a fundamental reset. As of July 2020, a stark reality set in for business leaders worldwide: adapt your model or face becoming obsolete. The pandemic exposed vulnerabilities in long-standing operations, forcing a moment of reckoning. From multinational corporations to local mainstays, the question was the same: how do we not only survive this crisis but also position ourselves for the future that emerges on the other side?

This chapter is a strategic guide for that very purpose. We will move beyond panic and into a framework for decisive action, outlining immediate steps to stabilize your business and a forward-looking analysis of the industries poised for growth in a post-pandemic world.

Part 1: The Crisis Management Playbook - Stabilizing Your Business

When the ground is shifting, a clear, methodical approach is your greatest asset. Here are the critical steps to secure your business's present to ensure it has a future.

1. Conduct a Financial Triage: Preserve Capital

Immediate survival hinges on cash flow. This is not the time for major investments or non-essential spending. Your primary focus must be:

- **Cash Flow Analysis:** Meticulously track every dollar coming in (revenue) and going out (expenses). Identify and eliminate any discretionary spending.
- **Liquidity is King:** Build your cash reserves. Delay capital expenditures, negotiate payment terms with creditors, and accelerate accounts receivable collections. Cash on hand is your buffer against uncertainty.
- **Minimize Risk:** Adopt a conservative financial posture until market stability returns.

2. Streamline for Efficiency: The Strategic Pivot

A crisis forces clarity. It reveals which parts of your business are core and which are draining resources.

- **Divest to Invest:** Critically evaluate all business units, product lines, and assets. If a segment is not producing revenue or is not aligned with your core mission, consider selling it off. This frees up capital and managerial focus for what truly matters.
- **Embrace Automation:** The digital age offers powerful tools to enhance efficiency and reduce dependency on manual processes. Analyze your operations, from customer service with chatbots to automated marketing and inventory management. The goal is to create a leaner, more resilient operation that can withstand future shocks by reducing fixed costs like extensive health and retirement benefits.

3. Strengthen Your Financial Position

Once you have controlled spending and streamlined operations, take a holistic view of your finances.

- **Balance the Books:** Ensure you have a clear, real-time understanding of your financial position. Know your net cash position after accounting for all liabilities.
- **Renegotiate Everything:** In a crisis, everyone is under pressure. Approach your vendors, landlords, and service providers to renegotiate terms. You may secure more favorable pricing or payment plans, improving your cash flow. Desperation can create opportunities for mutually beneficial deals.

4. Deepen Customer Relationships: Empathy as a Strategy

Your customers are the lifeblood of your business, and they are likely facing their own challenges. How you treat them now will define your brand for years to come.

- **Be a Solution, Not a Problem:** Proactively communicate with your customer base. Can you offer flexible payment plans, value-added services, or simply a message of understanding and support?
- **Build Loyalty:** Demonstrating empathy and providing genuine value during a difficult time fosters deep, lasting loyalty. Your customers will remember who stood by them.

A Sobering Statistic: The World Trade Organization (WTO) predicted global trade would fall by 13% to 32% in 2020. This underscores the profound, worldwide nature of the economic shock and the critical need for smart management.

Part 2: The Future-Proof Industries - Where Opportunity Lies

While some doors were closing, others were flung wide open. The pandemic accelerated certain societal trends, creating powerful tailwinds for specific sectors. The wealthy and well-informed are shifting their resources into these areas. Here's where to look for growth.

1. The Digital Infrastructure

The mass shift to remote work and online life supercharged everything digital.

- **E-Commerce & Digital Marketing:** With brick-and-mortar stores shuttered, the migration to online shopping became a stampede. Businesses with a strong digital presence thrived. Understanding SEO, social media advertising, and online customer acquisition is no longer optional; it's essential.
- **Remote Collaboration & Cloud Services:** Platforms that enable remote work (like Zoom, Slack, and Microsoft Teams) and cloud infrastructure (like AWS and Google Cloud) became the backbone of the global economy.
- **Cybersecurity:** As business moved online, the attack surface for cybercriminals expanded, creating massive demand for security solutions.

2. The Home-Centered Economy

With people spending unprecedented time at home, new consumption patterns emerged.

- **Streaming Entertainment:** Services like Netflix, Disney+, and HBO Max saw subscriber numbers soar as demand for home-based entertainment exploded.
- **The Gaming Industry:** From console platforms like PlayStation and Xbox to mobile and PC gaming, engagement and revenue reached new heights, solidifying gaming as a dominant form of entertainment.
- **Home Fitness & Wellness:** With gyms closed, digital fitness platforms (like Peloton and Mirror) and at-home workout equipment saw unprecedented demand, alongside a heightened focus on immune-boosting supplements and health products.

3. Essential and Adaptive Services

Certain needs became non-negotiable, while others adapted to new constraints.

- **Logistics & Last-Mile Delivery:** Companies like Amazon, UPS, and FedEx, as well as food delivery services like DoorDash and Instacart, became vital lifelines, and this reliance on hyper-convenient delivery is here to stay.
- **Online Education & Upskilling:** The closure of universities and corporate training rooms forced a rapid adoption of online learning. Platforms like **Coursera**, **Udemy**, and **edX** became crucial for students and professionals looking to adapt their skills for the new economy.
- **Telehealth & Medical Solutions:** The need for remote medical consultations and the massive demand for Personal Protective Equipment (PPE) created a boom in telehealth services and medical supply companies.

4. The Agile Workforce

The traditional employment model was disrupted, giving rise to more flexible structures.

The Freelance & Gig Economy: Companies seeking flexibility and specialized skills for short-term projects turned to freelancers. For highly skilled individuals, this represents an opportunity for autonomy and diverse income streams.

Conclusion: Building for What's Next

The post-pandemic world is not be a return to **"normal."** It is a new landscape, shaped by the lessons of the crisis. The businesses that thrived were those that used this time to become more efficient, more digital, and more customer-centric.

The industries outlined above are not fleeting trends; they are the foundation of the next decade of economic growth. By managing your current crisis with discipline and aligning your future with these growth sectors, you can do more than just survive future crisis that may be on the horizon, you can position your enterprise to emerge stronger, more resilient, and ready to lead in the new era.

Resource Directory: Tools for Adaptation and Growth

Financial Management & Crisis Guidance:

- **U.S. Small Business Administration (SBA):** `www.sba.gov` - For disaster loan information and general business guidance.
- **SCORE:** `www.score.org` - Free mentorship and business workshops from retired executives.

Automation & Digital Tools:

- **Zapier:** `www.zapier.com` - Automates workflows between different web apps.
- **HubSpot:** `www.hubspot.com` - Offers a suite of marketing, sales, and customer service automation tools.

Online Learning & Skill Development:

- **Coursera:** `www.coursera.org` - Courses and degrees from top universities.
- **edX:** `www.edx.org` - Similar to Coursera, with a wide range of university-backed courses.
- **Udemy:** `www.udemy.com` - A vast marketplace for practical, skills-based courses.

- **LinkedIn Learning:** `www.linkedin.com/learning` - Professional development courses integrated with your LinkedIn profile.
- **Khan Academy:** `www.khanacademy.org` - Excellent for free, foundational knowledge on a wide range of subjects.

Section 4

Online Business Success

Steps to a Winning Business

In The Digital Economy &

The Growing Trends

Chapter 26

Building Your Digital Empire

Your Blueprint for Online Business Success

Introduction

Embarking on the journey of starting an online business can feel overwhelming. With so many strategies, platforms, and technical terms, where do you even begin? This chapter is designed to demystify the process. Whether you're looking to sell a unique product, offer a specialized service, or share your expertise with the world, we will guide you through the essential, foundational steps to build a web business that is structured for success. We'll start with the core principles of planning and understanding your market, then move into the practical steps of setup and execution.

In this chapter, you will learn:

- How to craft a strategic plan for your website's success.
- The critical importance of knowing your target customer inside and out.
- How to set defined, measurable goals for your online venture.
- Strategies for developing a realistic promotions budget.
- How to honestly assess your own skills and when it's time to seek help.
- An overview of the digital marketing landscape and proven ways to generate revenue online.

The Pillars of a Successful Online Business

Success on the internet isn't accidental; it's built. The **"absolute best way to success,"** as you rightly noted, is through a controlled, step-by-step process. Think of your business as a house, it needs a solid foundation and strong supporting pillars.

Pillar 1: Strategy & Customer Insight (The Plan)

Before you write a single line of code or design a logo, you must answer the fundamental strategic questions.

- **Understanding Your Customer & Competition:** Who are you selling to? What problem do they have that you can solve? Use the internet to research your competitors. If you sell handmade leather bags, search for others in your space. Analyze their websites, their customer reviews, and their social media presence. Tools like **SEMrush** or **Ahrefs** can provide deep insights into your competitors' traffic and keywords.

- **Defining Your Value Proposition:** Does your product or service offer a genuine solution or create a positive feeling? People buy to fulfill needs, often categorized as Physiological, Safety, Love/Belonging, Esteem, and Self-Actualization. Aligning your offer with one of these core needs dramatically increases your chance of making a sale.
- **Establishing Clear Goals & Budget:** Vague goals like **"Make Money"** are not actionable. Instead, ask:
  - What is my desired annual revenue? ($50,000? $100,000?)
  - How many sales per month does that require, based on my average product price?
  - What is my working budget for marketing and operations?

Pillar 2: Execution & Infrastructure (The Setup)

This is where your plan meets the real world. You need to build and control your digital assets.

- **Your Digital Headquarters: The Website:** Your website is your 24/7 storefront, sales team, and support desk. It must be professional, easy to use, and cost-effective. Unlike a physical store, your online presence can compete globally and is always open for business.
- **Controlling Your Digital Keys:** You must maintain control over all your accounts and data. This includes:
  - Domain name registration
  - Web hosting and email accounts
  - Website files and design sources
  - Social media and advertising account

Recommended Tool: Use a password manager to securely store all this information. Options include **1Password**, **LastPass**, or **Dashlane**.

Pillar 3: Growth & Scaling (The Expansion)

Once your foundation is solid and your business is running, the focus shifts to growth.

- **Driving Targeted Traffic:** Your most important job is to attract visitors. This can be done through:
  - **SEO (Search Engine Optimization):** Getting free traffic from Google.
  - **Social Media Marketing:** Engaging audiences on platforms like Instagram, Facebook, or TikTok.
  - **Content Marketing:** Creating valuable blog posts, videos, or podcasts that attract people searching for answers.

    - **Paid Advertising:** Using platforms like Google Ads or social media ads to get immediate, targeted traffic.
- **Building Your Team:** You can't do it all alone. Recognize your strengths and outsource your weaknesses. This could mean hiring a freelance graphic designer, a copywriter, or, most powerfully, building a sales force through an **Affiliate Program**. Affiliates promote your products for a commission, dramatically expanding your reach.
- **Forging Strategic Partnerships:** A **Joint Venture (JV)** involves partnering with another business or influencer to promote to each other's audiences. A successful JV can expose your brand to thousands of new potential customers overnight.

Your Actionable Launch Plan

Let's break down the foundational steps into a clear, actionable checklist.

Step 1: Secure Your Digital Assets

Protect your business from the start. Use a password manager to organize your login information for your domain registrar (e.g., GoDaddy, Namecheap), hosting provider (e.g., SiteGround, Bluehost), and other critical services.

Step 2: Define Your Offer & Delivery Method

What are you selling? A physical product, a digital download, a coaching service? How will you get it to the customer? (e.g., shipping, instant download). How will you get paid? (e.g., Stripe, PayPal, Shopify Payments). Answer these questions in detail before you build your site.

Step 3: Validate Your Solution

Ask yourself critically: **"Does my product/service solve a real problem or fulfill a deep desire for a specific group of people?"** Your marketing will be far more effective if you are conveying a solution, not just listing features.

Step 4: Craft Your Traffic Generation Strategy

Don't just hope for traffic; plan for it. Decide on one or two primary methods to start.

- **For organic reach:** Start a blog using https://wordpress.org and learn SEO.
- **For paid traffic:** Set a small initial budget to test platforms like **Google Ads** or **Meta Ads Manager**.
- **For influencer-driven traffic:** Research potential partners in your niche.

Step 5: Establish Your Authority

Become the go-to expert in your field by sharing your knowledge. Start a blog, a YouTube channel, or a podcast. Consistently providing value builds trust, and people buy from those they trust.

Step 6: Build Your Support Network

Plan for growth by identifying where you'll need help.

- **For Affiliate Programs:** Platforms like **ShareASale**, **ClickBank**, or built-in tools like **Shopify Affiliates** can help you manage a network of promoters.
- **For Freelance Help:** Sites like **Upwork** or **Fiverr** connect you with skilled professionals for specific tasks like web design, writing, or video editing.

Step 7: Seek Strategic Alliances

Look for non-competing businesses that serve the same target audience as you. Propose a collaborative webinar, a bundled product offering, or a simple cross-promotion to tap into their established customer base.

Key Takeaways & Moving Forward

Running a successful online business requires you to wear many hats: strategist, marketer, and CEO. The most critical skill you can develop is the ability to make data-driven decisions. Use the formulas provided to understand your conversion rates and set realistic traffic goals. Monitor your progress, be ready to adapt, and don't be afraid to invest in expert help to overcome obstacles.

The digital world moves quickly, but a business built on a solid foundation of planning, customer understanding, and strategic execution is built to last. In the following chapters, we will dive deeper into each of these pillars, giving you the advanced tools you need to thrive.

Recommended Resources for Further Learning:

- **For Business Setup & E-commerce:** https://www.shopifyacademy.com
- **For Digital Marketing Education:** https://academy.hubspot.com (Free courses and certifications)
- **For SEO & Content Marketing:** https://backlinko.com (Advanced strategies and guides)
- **For Industry Trends & News:** https://www.searchenginejournal.com

Chapter 27

Securing Your Digital Empire with Artificial Intelligence

Smart Steps and AI Tools to Launch and Manage Your Online Business

The internet has leveled the playing field for entrepreneurs. What once required office space, a large team, and significant capital can now be accomplished with a laptop, a Wi-Fi connection, and a clear vision. The rise of artificial intelligence (AI) and easy-to-use web platforms has made it possible for anyone, regardless of technical experience, to build a thriving online business from the ground up.

In this chapter, we'll explore how to create your online presence, use AI to accelerate your success, and manage your business efficiently in the digital world. Whether your goal is to sell products, promote services, or share your expertise, these tools and strategies will help you build a strong and sustainable digital empire.

Laying the Foundation: Your Online Identity

Every successful online business starts with a solid foundation, a website. Think of your website as your digital storefront. It's the first impression most customers will have of you, and it should reflect professionalism, trust, and purpose.

Your first step is to secure a **domain name**, the unique web address where visitors can find you. Choose something that's easy to spell, memorable, and clearly connected to your brand or business idea. Popular and reputable domain registrars include

- Namecheap **https://www.namecheap.com/hosting**
- Google Domains: **https://domains.google**
- GoDaddy: **https://www.godaddy.com**

Once your domain is registered, you'll need **web hosting**, which is essentially the online "land" your site will live on.

Reliable hosting providers include:

- Bluehost: **https://www.bluehost.com**
- SiteGround: **https://www.siteground.com**
- Hostinger: **https://www.hostinger.com**

For WordPress sites,

WPEngine: https://wpengine.com is a premium option that offers speed and security.

Designing Your Website: AI-Powered Simplicity

In the early days of the internet, building a website meant learning code or hiring a web developer. Today, that's no longer the case. Thanks to **AI-powered website builders**, creating a sleek, functional, and mobile-friendly site is faster and easier than ever.

Tools like **Wix ADI** and **Durable.co** can generate a complete website in minutes simply by asking you a few questions about your business. They automatically design your layout, write your initial content, and suggest images that fit your brand.

If you prefer WordPress, platforms like **10Web.io:** https://10web.io can use AI to clone or enhance existing sites and automate updates. Other excellent options such as: **Shopify Magic**: https://www.shopify.com/magic offer built-in AI tools to create copy, choose color palettes, and optimize your layout for conversions.

By using AI, you not only save time but also gain access to professional-grade design and branding features that would otherwise cost thousands of dollars.

Creating Engaging Content: Let AI Help You Tell Your Story

Your website is your foundation, but **content** is what drives people to it. From blog posts and product descriptions to videos and social media updates, great content builds trust, showcases your expertise, and attracts loyal customers.

Artificial intelligence has become an indispensable ally in this area. Tools like **ChatGPT:** https://chatgpt.com , **Jasper AI:** https://www.jasper.ai , and **Copy.ai:** https://www.copy.ai can generate blog posts, email campaigns, and landing page copy in seconds. They can help you brainstorm article ideas, refine your messaging, or even rewrite existing content for better clarity and SEO performance.

Visual content is just as important. **Canva:** https://www.canva.com lets you design professional-quality graphics with AI-driven suggestions for layout and color coordination, while **Pictory.ai:** https://pictory.ai can transform written articles into engaging videos perfect for YouTube or social media.

By leveraging these tools, you can maintain a consistent online presence without spending endless hours on content creation.

Setting Up Shop: Selling Online with Ease

If your goal is to sell products or services, integrating an **e-commerce system** into your website is essential. Fortunately, there are many beginner-friendly platforms to help you do this.

Shopify: https://www.shopify.com remains one of the most popular all-in-one solutions for product-based businesses. It handles everything from inventory management to payment processing. For WordPress users, **WooCommerce:** https://woocommerce.com is a free plugin that adds a full online store to your site. Creatives and artisans often thrive on **Etsy:** https://www.etsy.com/sell , while those who want design-driven templates may prefer **Squarespace Commerce**: https://www.squarespace.com

When it comes to accepting payments, options like **Stripe:** https://stripe.com , **PayPal Business:** https://www.paypal.com/business , and **Square:** https://squareup.com/us/en make it easy to receive funds securely from anywhere in the world. These platforms integrate directly into most website builders, so setup is quick and intuitive.

Running Your Business with AI Efficiency

Running a business online involves juggling multiple tasks, customer service, marketing, analytics, and more. This is where AI shines brightest.

To streamline communication, AI chatbots like **Tidio**: https://www.tidio.com and **Intercom** : https://www.intercom.com can answer customer questions 24/7. For managing marketing campaigns, **HubSpot**: https://www.hubspot.com offers an all-in-one CRM system with built-in AI to track leads, automate emails, and generate insights about your audience.

Analytics platforms such as **Google Analytics 4** and **Surfer SEO** can help you understand visitor behavior, optimize your content, and boost your ranking on search engines. For workflow automation, **Zapier**: https://zapier.com connects your favorite apps, such as Gmail, Slack, and Shopify, so tasks like sending invoices or following up with customers happen automatically.

To keep your business organized, **Notion AI:** https://www.notion.com/product/ai and **ClickUp AI**: https://clickup.com/brain can manage your to-do lists, create content outlines, and summarize data, giving you more time to focus on growth.

Promoting Your Online Presence

Once your site is live, you'll need to attract visitors and convert them into loyal customers. This is where digital marketing, and AI-enhanced promotion, becomes essential.

Use **Lumen5**: https://lumen5.com to create short video ads from your written content, or **AdCreative.ai**: https://www.adcreative.ai to automatically generate high-performing social media ads. Platforms like **Hootsuite**: https://www.hootsuite.com and **Buffer**:

https://buffer.com let you schedule posts across multiple channels, while **Mailchimp**: https://mailchimp.com uses AI to personalize email campaigns and analyze open rates.

Consistent and intelligent marketing ensures that your business not only launches successfully but continues to grow over time.

Keep Learning: Staying Ahead in the Digital Economy

The online business world evolves constantly, and ongoing education is your greatest asset. Fortunately, there are excellent (and often free) resources to help you stay current.

- **Coursera**: https://www.coursera.org and **Udemy**: https://www.udemy.com offer affordable courses on web development, marketing, and entrepreneurship.
- **Google Digital Garage**: https://grow.google provides free lessons in SEO, analytics, and e-commerce.
- **HubSpot Academy**: https://academy.hubspot.com teaches digital marketing, social media strategy, and CRM management at no cost.

Continuous learning ensures that you can adapt as new technologies, algorithms, and marketing trends emerge.

Final Thoughts: The Smart Way to Build an Online Business

Creating a web-based business no longer requires deep technical expertise or a large investment. AI has made it possible for anyone with a clear idea and commitment to success to build, manage, and grow a business online.

Start by establishing your online foundation, then let artificial intelligence help you design your website, generate compelling content, and streamline your daily operations. Automate what you can, learn constantly, and focus on connecting authentically with your audience.

With the right mindset, the right tools, and a willingness to evolve, your online business can become more than a website, it can become your digital empire.

Chapter 28

Converting Visitors into Customers & Knowing When to Bring in the Pros

This chapter focuses on the core objective of your online business: transforming anonymous website traffic into a loyal customer base and generating revenue. We will explore the essential tools and strategies for capturing leads, building trust, and guiding visitors toward a purchase. Furthermore, we'll provide a clear framework for deciding when to handle tasks yourself and when to invest in professional help to scale your operations effectively.

The Art of the Capture: Turning Traffic into Prospects

Simply having a website is not enough. Your primary goal is to engage visitors and convert them into potential prospects, leads you can nurture into paying customers. This conversion process hinges on strategic points of contact that make it easy for visitors to take the next step.

Strategic Contact Forms: Your Digital Handshake

A contact form is more than just a box for an email; it's a guided action. It's a critical tool for initiating contact, growing your email list, qualifying leads, and gathering valuable customer insights.

While a simple **"Name, Email, Message"** form works for general inquiries, different goals require specialized forms:

1. **Contact Form:** For general questions and customer service inquiries.
2. **Lead Generation Form:** The workhorse of online marketing. Used to offer a valuable resource (e.g., an ebook, webinar, or discount code) in exchange for contact information.
3. **Order Form:** The final step in the sales process, designed for seamless and secure transactions.
4. **Event Registration Form:** For signing up for webinars, workshops, or live events.
5. **Feedback/Survey Form:** To gather customer opinions, conduct market research, and improve your services.

Best Practices for High-Converting Forms:

- **Less is More:** Limit fields to only what is absolutely necessary. The more you ask, the higher the abandonment rate.

- **Contextual Fields:** Use smart forms that reveal additional fields based on previous user input to avoid overwhelming visitors.
- **Clarity and Guidance:** Use clear labels, placeholder text, and error messages. For multiple-choice options, use radio buttons or checkboxes.
- **Visual Design:** The form should match your site's branding and color scheme to feel like a natural part of the user experience.
- **Build Trust:** If you're asking for sensitive data, link to your privacy policy. Explain why you need the information.
- **Strategic Placement:** Position forms where they are highly visible and contextually relevant, such as at the end of a blog post or on a dedicated landing page.

Recommended Form Builder Platforms:

These services offer drag-and-drop builders, templates, and integrations with other marketing tools.

- **Jotform** (https://www.jotform.com)
- **Formstack** (https://www.formstack.com)
- **Google Forms** (https://workspace.google.com/products/forms) - A robust and free option from Google.
- **Typeform** (https://www.typeform.com) - Known for its conversational, user-friendly forms.

The Power of Live Chat: Instant Engagement

While phone support is traditional, it's costly and inefficient. Live chat offers a modern solution, allowing your team to assist multiple visitors simultaneously, which cuts costs and boosts satisfaction.

Key Benefits of Live Chat:

- **Immediate Resolution:** Customers get answers in real-time, reducing frustration.
- **Increased Conversions:** Intervene with hesitant shoppers by answering last-minute questions, directly leading to more sales.
- **Proactive Lead Generation:** Reach out to visitors who have been on a page for a long time, offering assistance.
- **Competitive Advantage:** Provides a level of personal service that sets you apart.

- **Modern Live Chat & Customer Service Platforms:**

- **Zendesk** (https://www.zendesk.com) - A full-suite customer service platform.
- **Intercom** (https://www.intercom.com) - Excellent for marketing, sales, and support with a focus on customer messaging.
- **Freshdesk** (https://www.freshworks.com/freshdesk) - A user-friendly helpdesk with robust live chat features.
- **Tidio** (https://www.tidio.com) - A popular and affordable option for small businesses.

Driving Traffic: The Role of Social Media

Your website and social media profiles are intrinsically linked. Visitors will often check your social media to gauge your credibility, activity, and community engagement. A strong social media presence is non-negotiable for building a following and driving consistent traffic back to your site.

A Strategic Approach to Key Platforms:

- **Facebook:** Ideal for building community, sharing blog posts, running targeted ads, and fostering personal connections with your audience. Use it to tell your brand's story.
- **Twitter/X:** Perfect for real-time engagement, sharing quick updates, industry news, and participating in relevant conversations. It's a powerful tool for customer service and direct communication.
- **LinkedIn:** The premier network for B2B marketing. Establish your authority by joining industry groups, publishing articles on LinkedIn Pulse, and connecting with other professionals.
- **Instagram & Pinterest:** Visual platforms that are highly effective for lifestyle, fashion, food, art, and design businesses. Use high-quality images, Stories, and Reels to showcase your products and inspire your audience.
- **YouTube:** As the second largest search engine, YouTube is essential for video marketing. Create educational tutorials, product demonstrations, or behind-the-scenes content to build authority and trust.

Social Media Management Tools:

To streamline your efforts, consider using tools like **Buffer** (https://buffer.com), **Hootsuite** (https://www.hootsuite.com), or **Later** (https://later.com) to schedule posts, monitor engagement, and analyze performance across multiple platforms from a single dashboard.

Scaling Your Business: Building Your Digital Team

As your business grows, you'll reach a point where your time is better spent on strategy than on execution. Knowing when and how to hire help is critical for sustainable growth.

When to Hire an Internet Marketing Expert or Web Service Provider

Consider bringing in pros when:

- Your technical skills are limiting your website's functionality or design.
- You lack the time to execute a consistent marketing strategy.
- You need specialized expertise (e.g., SEO, paid advertising) that you don't possess.
- The time you spend on tasks is more valuable than the cost of outsourcing them.

Building Your Core Digital Team

You don't need to hire full-time employees immediately. You can build a team of freelancers and agencies for specific roles:

- **Website Designer/Developer:** Creates a fast, secure, and responsive website that provides an excellent user experience.
- **Content Creator/Copywriter:** Develops engaging blog posts, website copy, and product descriptions that attract and convert visitors.
- **SEO/SEM Specialist:** Optimizes your site to rank higher in organic search results and manages paid advertising campaigns (like Google Ads).
- **Social Media Manager:** Develops strategy, creates content, and engages with your community across all platforms.

How to Choose the Right Partner or Vendor

Selecting the right provider is a business-critical decision. Follow these steps to ensure a good fit:

1. **Define Your Goals & Budget:** Be clear about what you want to achieve and how much you can invest.
2. **Review Portfolios and Case Studies:** Look for proven experience in your industry or with similar projects.
3. **Check Reviews and Testimonials:** Sites like https://clutch.co or Google My Business can provide unbiased feedback.
4. **Conduct a Thorough Interview:** Prepare a list of questions, such as:

    - **"What is your process for a project like mine?"**
    - **"How do you measure and report on success?"**
    - **"What is your typical communication cadence?"**
    - **"Can you provide references from past clients?"**

5. **Discuss Logistics:** Clarify pricing (hourly vs. project-based), timelines, and what happens if the project scope changes.

Top Freelance & Service Marketplaces

- **Upwork** (https://www.upwork.com) - A massive marketplace for freelancers in every discipline.
- **Fiverr** (https://www.fiverr.com) - Great for finding affordable, specific "gigs."
- **Toptal** (https://www.toptal.com) - A curated network of the top 3% of freelance talent.
- **99designs** (https://99designs.com) - Specializes in connecting you with talented designers through contests or direct hiring.

Conclusion: Your Path to Strategic Growth

The journey from a website visitor to a loyal customer is built on strategic engagement, through intuitive forms, instant communication, and valuable social content. By mastering these elements, you lay a strong foundation for growth.

Recognize that your role as a business owner is to be the strategist and visionary. Knowing when to delegate technical, creative, or marketing tasks to skilled professionals is not a sign of weakness, but a strategic move that frees you to focus on scaling your business. Assess your strengths, acknowledge your limitations, and build a team that complements your skills, empowering you to achieve your business goals more efficiently and effectively.

Chapter 29

The Digital Revenue Engine

Monetizing Your Online Presence

Introduction: The Mindset for Online Income

The journey to making money online is often portrayed as a get-rich-quick scheme, but the reality is more subtle. While some struggle for years without significant results, others build sustainable, profitable businesses. The key difference isn't luck; it's a combination of strategy, value creation, and understanding the digital landscape. This chapter will demystify the process, introducing you to proven monetization models, essential tools, and strategic approaches to turn your website and audience into a reliable revenue engine.

Core Monetization Models: Choosing Your Path

Before you begin, the most critical question to ask is: **What value do I provide?** Your online income will be built on solving a problem, teaching a skill, or appealing to a passion. Once you identify your core value, you can align it with one or more of these primary monetization models:

1. **Selling Your Own Products & Services:** The pinnacle of control and profit potential.
2. **Affiliate Marketing:** Earning commissions by promoting other companies' products.
3. **Content & Blogging Monetization:** Leveraging your expertise and audience through various formats.
4. **Advertising Revenue:** Generating income from the traffic visiting your site.

Selling Your Own Products & Services

This model offers the highest degree of creative control and the potential for exponential growth, as you keep all profits after expenses.

Key Product Categories to Consider:

- **Digital Information Products:** These are low-cost, high-margin items that leverage your knowledge.

- **E-books & Guides:** Package your expertise into a downloadable PDF. Platforms like **Google Docs** or **Canva** can help with design.
- **Online Courses:** Create a structured learning experience. Use platforms like **Teachable**, **Thinkific**, or **Kajabi** to host and sell your courses.
- **Membership Sites:** Offer exclusive content, communities, or services for a recurring fee. Platforms like **Mighty Networks** or **MemberPress** are ideal for this.
- **Audio & Video Products:** Engage your audience with rich media.
- **Podcasts:** Monetize through sponsorships, paid subscriptions, or by using the show to promote your other products. Use **Buzzsprout** or **Anchor** for hosting.
- **Premium Video Content:** Create in-depth tutorials, documentaries, or entertainment. Host on **Vimeo On Demand** or use **Wistia** for business-focused video.
- **Webinars & Online Workshops:** Offer live, interactive training. These can be sold as ticketed events and then repurposed into recorded products for ongoing income.
- **Recommended Platforms: Zoom Webinars**, **Demio**, and **WebinarJam**.
- **Physical & Handmade Goods:** Turn a craft or passion into a business.
- **Benefits:** You work with products you love, on your own schedule, and can build a loyal customer base.
- **Recommended Marketplaces: Etsy** (for handmade and vintage), **Big Cartel** (for artists and makers), or your own website powered by **Shopify** or **Squarespace**.

Harnessing the Power of Affiliate Marketing

Affiliate marketing involves promoting another company's product. You earn a commission for every sale or action generated through your unique referral link. It's powerful because you don't have to handle product creation, inventory, or customer service.

The Affiliate Process, Simplified:

- **Find a Relevant Program:** Choose products you genuinely believe in that align with your audience's interests.
- **Join an Affiliate Network:** These are hubs that connect publishers (you) with advertisers.
    - **ShareASale** and **Commission Junction (CJ)**: Large networks with thousands of brands.
    - **ClickBank:** Specializes in digital information products like e-books and software.
    - **Amazon Associates:** A great starting point due to its vast product range, though commissions are typically lower.
- **Promote Your Links Ethically:** Integrate your affiliate links into blog posts, product reviews, email newsletters, and social media. Always disclose your affiliate relationships to maintain trust.

Monetizing Content and Blogging

A blog is not just a journal; it's the foundation of your online authority. Once you have a steady stream of readers, you can monetize through:

- **Selling Digital Products:** As mentioned above, your blog is the perfect platform to sell your e-books, courses, or templates.
- **Display Advertising:** Use networks like **Google AdSense** or **Mediavine** (for larger sites) to place ads on your site. You earn when visitors view or click the ads.
- **Sponsored Content:** Companies pay you to write a post or create content featuring their product.
- **Freelance Writing & Consulting:** Use your blog as a portfolio to attract clients for your writing or consulting services.

Getting Started with a Blog:

For a comprehensive guide, **ProBlogger** is an invaluable resource. The essential steps are: choosing a platform like **WordPress**, securing hosting from a provider like **SiteGround** or **Bluehost**, and consistently creating valuable content for your target audience.

Converting Traffic into Cash with Advertising

If you have significant website traffic, you can monetize it directly through ad placements.

- **Google AdSense:** The most common entry-level ad network. It's easy to set up but offers less control over the ads displayed.
- **Direct Ad Sales & Sponsorships:** Sell banner ad space directly to relevant brands. This often commands a higher price than passive networks.
- **Understanding Ad Models:**
  - **CPC (Cost-Per-Click):** You earn money each time a visitor clicks an ad.
  - **CPM (Cost-Per-Mille):** You earn money for every 1,000 impressions (views) an ad receives.
  - **CPA (Cost-Per-Action):** You earn a commission only when a user takes a specific action, like making a purchase or signing up for a trial.

The Engine Room: Building a Seamless Buying Process

A brilliant product and traffic are useless if your buying process is broken. A successful online transaction relies on three core components:

1. **The Transaction Page (Shopping Cart):** This is where the purchase happens. It must be clear, simple, and secure. Solutions like **Shopify**, **WooCommerce** (for WordPress), or **ThriveCart** provide robust, user-friendly cart experiences.

2. **The Merchant Account:** This is a special bank account that allows you to accept credit card payments. Services like **PayPal**, **Stripe**, and **Square** have simplified this process immensely.
3. **The Payment Gateway:** This is the technology that securely transmits the customer's payment information between the shopping cart and the merchant account. Often, services like Stripe and PayPal act as both the gateway and the merchant account.

Crucial Checkout Best Practices:

- Build trust by displaying security badges (SSL certificates).
- Offer multiple payment options (Credit Card, PayPal, Apple Pay).
- Be transparent about shipping costs and delivery times.
- Remove all unnecessary navigation from the checkout page to prevent cart abandonment.

Strategic Upselling: Maximizing Customer Value

Increase your average order value by strategically offering complementary products.

- **Up-selling:** Encouraging the customer to buy a premium version of what they're already purchasing (e.g., **"Upgrade to the Deluxe Package for $30 more**").
- **Cross-selling:** Suggesting related products that complement the purchase (e.g., **"Customers who bought this camera also bought this lens cleaning kit").**
- **Back-end Selling:** Offering additional products *after* the initial purchase is complete, often via email. This could be an advanced course, a one-on-one consultation, or a physical book that complements their digital purchase.

Fueling the Engine: Driving Targeted Traffic

Your revenue engine needs fuel, that fuel is traffic. A multi-channel approach is essential:

- **Search Engine Optimization (SEO):** Optimize your content to rank higher in Google search results. This is a long-term, sustainable strategy. Use tools like **Ahrefs Webmaster Tools** (free) or **SEMrush** for insights.
- **Content Marketing & Blogging:** Create valuable, problem-solving content that attracts and retains a clearly defined audience.
- **Social Media Marketing:** Promote your content and build community on platforms where your target audience spends time (e.g., **Pinterest** for visual topics, **LinkedIn** for B2B, **TikTok/Instagram** for younger demographics).
- **Email Marketing:** Build an email list from day one. It's your most owned and valuable marketing channel. Use services like **ConvertKit** or **Mailchimp** to manage your list and send newsletters.

- **Paid Advertising:** Use **Google Ads** or **Meta Ads** to get immediate, targeted traffic. This requires a budget but can yield quick results.

Scaling Your Empire: Affiliate Programs & Joint Ventures

Once you have a successful product, you can scale your reach by getting others to sell for you.

- **Creating Your Own Affiliate Program:**

1. Have a great product that people want to promote.
2. Use a platform like **ShareASale**, **Refersion**, or **Tapfiliate** to manage your affiliates, track sales, and issue payments.
3. Actively recruit and support your affiliates with marketing materials and competitive commissions.

- **Forming a Joint Venture (JV):** Partner with a non-competing business that shares your target audience. They promote your product to their email list or audience for a share of the revenue. This provides instant access to a new, trusted customer base.

Conclusion: Building Your Sustainable Digital Business

Making money online is a marathon, not a sprint. It requires patience, testing, and a relentless focus on providing value. Evaluate the models discussed here, selling your own products, affiliate marketing, content creation, and advertising, and determine which best aligns with your skills, resources, and audience. Start with one, master it, and then strategically layer in others to build a diverse and resilient digital revenue engine for your business.

Chapter 30

Mastering the Digital Marketplace

A Strategic Guide to SEO & Web Analytics

Introduction: The Engine of Online Discovery

Every time you type a query into Google or Bing, you're initiating a digital race. The websites that appear on the first page aren't there by accident; they have mastered the art and science of Search Engine Optimization (SEO). This chapter will demystify SEO, transforming it from a buzzword into a practical, actionable strategy for driving targeted traffic to your website, building brand authority, and ultimately growing your business.

The first and most critical lesson is that SEO is a marathon, not a sprint. It requires patience, consistency, and a commitment to quality. The rewards, however, are substantial: sustained, organic growth that builds a foundation for long-term success.

The Search Engine Landscape: Where Your Customers Are

While Google is the undeniable giant, capturing over 90% of the global search market share, understanding the broader ecosystem is valuable. Different engines cater to different audiences and intents.

Google Website Tool: https://search.google.com/search-console/about?hl=en

- **Google:** The primary focus for most SEO strategies. Its algorithms set the standard for relevance and user experience.
- **Bing & Yahoo:** Still command a significant user base, often integrated into Microsoft Windows and older email portals. A well-optimized site will typically perform well on both.
- **Niche and Regional Engines:**

  Baidu: Dominates the Chinese market. Essential for businesses targeting customers in China.

  Yandex: The leading search engine in Russia.

DuckDuckGo: Has grown significantly as a privacy-focused alternative that doesn't track user data.

Key Takeaway: Your primary strategy should be built for Google, but ensure your site is technically sound to be properly indexed by all major engines.

How Search Engines Work: The Bots, The Crawl, and The Index

To rank well, you must understand the process. Search engines use automated software called **bots** or **spiders** to **crawl** the billions of pages on the web. They follow links from one page to another, reading the content they find.

This information is then stored in a massive database called the **index**. When a user performs a search, the engine's algorithm sifts through the index to find the most **relevant** and authoritative pages, ranking them in order of perceived value.

Your goal is simple: make your website easy to crawl, easy to understand, and packed with value so the algorithm sees it as the best possible answer.

The Pillars of Modern SEO: How to Rank Higher

SEO can be broken down into three core pillars. Success requires a balanced approach across all of them.

Technical SEO: The Foundation

This is about the backend health of your website. If your site is slow or broken, nothing else matters.

- **Site Speed:** A critical ranking factor. Use **Google PageSpeed Insights** to test and get recommendations.
- **Mobile-First Indexing:** Google primarily uses the mobile version of your site for indexing and ranking. A responsive, mobile-friendly design is non-negotiable.
- **Sitemap.xml:** This file acts as a roadmap for search engines, ensuring they don't miss any important pages.
- **Site Structure & URL:** A clean, logical URL structure (e.g., `yoursite.com/services/seo-consulting`) is easier for both users and bots to understand.

On-Page SEO: The Content

This is about optimizing the content and HTML source code of your pages.

- **Title Tags:** The most important on-page element. It's the blue clickable link in search results. Make it compelling and include your target keyword.

- **Meta Descriptions:** The snippet of text under the title tag. While not a direct ranking factor, it heavily influences click-through rates.
- **Headings (H1, H2, H3):** Use these to structure your content. Your main title should be an H1, with subheadings as H2s, etc. This provides a clear outline for readers and bots.
- **Content Quality: This is king.** Your content must be original, informative, and thoroughly answer the user's search query. **E-E-A-T** (Experience, Expertise, Authoritativeness, Trustworthiness) is a core concept for Google.
- **Internal Linking:** Linking to other relevant pages on your site helps distribute authority and keeps users engaged.

Off-Page SEO: The Reputation

This is about your website's reputation and authority in the broader internet, primarily measured through backlinks.

- **Backlinks:** Links from other high-quality, reputable websites to yours are like votes of confidence. Earning these naturally through creating exceptional content is the best strategy.

Essential SEO Toolbox: Your Guides to Data

You cannot manage what you cannot measure. These tools provide the data you need to make intelligent decisions.

- **Google Search Console (formerly Webmaster Tools): This is essential and free.** It shows you how Google sees your site, your search rankings, click-through rates, and any technical issues that need fixing.
- **Google Analytics:** The cornerstone of web analytics. It reveals who your visitors are, how they found you, and what they do on your site.
- **Google Keyword Planner:** (Within Google Ads) Excellent for researching search volume and competition for keywords.
- **Ahrefs Webmaster Tools:** A powerful new **free** tool that provides incredible data on your backlinks and organic keywords, similar to their premium products.
- **Semrush, Ahrefs (Premium), & Moz:** Industry-leading premium suites that offer comprehensive data on your site and your competitors'. They are investments, but invaluable for serious businesses.

Keyword Strategy: Speaking Your Customer's Language

Keywords are the bridge between your customers' questions and your answers. Effective keyword research goes beyond single words to focus on **user intent**.

- **Think in Phrases, Not Words:** Instead of **"shoes,"** target **"best running shoes for flat feet" or "vegan leather boots."**

- **Understand Intent:** Is the user looking to learn ("how to fix a leaky faucet"), to find a specific site ("Home Depot"), or to buy ("buy black converse online")? Your content must match the intent.
- **Use the Tools:** Leverage **Google Keyword Planner**, **Semrush's Keyword Magic Tool**, or **Ahrefs' Keywords Explorer** to discover valuable terms with a balance of high search volume and achievable competition.

Competitive Intelligence: Learning from the Leaders

In SEO, your competitors are your teachers. Use tools like **Semrush**, **SpyFu**, and **Ahrefs** to:

- See which keywords are driving traffic to their sites.
- Analyze their backlink profile to see who is linking to them.
- Identify content gaps, topics they rank for that you have not yet covered.

- Your goal isn't to copy, but to understand, then innovate and create something even better.

Structuring for Success: Content Clusters and User Experience

Modern SEO favors topic authority over isolated pages. A **content cluster** model organizes your website to demonstrate deep expertise on a subject.

1. **Choose a Core Topic:** (e.g., **"Keto Diet"**).
2. **Create a Pillar Page:** A comprehensive, high-level guide to the main topic.
3. **Develop Cluster Content:** Create more specific articles (e.g., **"Keto Breakfast Ideas," "Keto for Beginners," "Keto Snacks")** that all hyperlink back to the main pillar page.

This structure creates a silo of relevance that search engines love, and it provides a seamless, logical experience for your visitors, helping them find the information they need.

Conclusion: Your Path to SEO Success

SEO is not a one-time task but an ongoing cycle of creating, optimizing, measuring, and refining. It is the core of a sustainable online presence. Start by fixing the technical basics of your website, then build a content strategy rooted in keyword research and user intent. Use your analytics to guide your efforts, and always keep the user experience at the forefront.

The path may seem complex, but by implementing these strategies stage by stage, you will build a website that both search engines and customers trust. If the process becomes overwhelming, don't hesitate to hire a professional SEO consultant to help accelerate your journey to the top of the search results.

Chapter 31

Future-Proof Your Income

Building a Sustainable Online Career in the Digital Age

Introduction: The Mindset for Digital Success

The landscape of work has undergone a seismic shift. The traditional 9-to-5 career path is no longer the only, or even the most lucrative, route to financial security and personal fulfillment. The digital economy, accelerated by global events and rapid technological advancement, has opened a world of opportunity for those willing to adapt.

But success online isn't just about picking a trendy business model. It begins with a fundamental question: **What is your "Why"?**

Before you invest time and energy, you must define your purpose. This clarity will be the compass that guides your entire journey.

- **The Quick Cash Seeker:** Are you solely focused on generating income by any means necessary, with no particular passion?
- **The Legacy Builder:** Is your goal to build long-term wealth and security for yourself and your family?
- **The Value Creator:** Do you want to build a business that genuinely helps others, solves a problem, or makes a positive impact?
- **The Passion Pioneer:** Are you turning a hobby or deep interest into a sustainable income stream?

Your answer is critical. It will shape your business plan, your brand voice, and your resilience during the inevitable challenges. Document this purpose in a clear business plan. This plan is your blueprint, it should outline your vision, target audience, marketing strategies, and financial projections.

Furthermore, the ultimate goal of any modern online venture should be to develop **multiple streams of income**. This creates a resilient financial foundation, allowing you to weather market fluctuations and build wealth that isn't dependent on a single source.

Part 1: The Digital Gold Rush: Top Online Business Models for 2025 and Beyond

Here are some of the most powerful and sustainable ways to generate income online.

1. Affiliate Marketing: Earning by Endorsement

Affiliate marketing is the art of promoting other companies' products or services. You earn a commission for every sale or action generated through your unique referral link.

- **The Key to Success:** This isn't about spamming links. Success comes from building trust with an audience. You must create high-quality content—reviews, tutorials, blog posts—that adds genuine value and directs qualified traffic to a solution you believe in. Patience is essential, as building an audience takes time.
- **Best Platforms to Start:**

  ShareASale (`www.shareasale.com`): A massive network with thousands of merchants.

  ClickBank (`www.clickbank.com`): Focuses heavily on digital products like e-books and online courses.

  Amazon Associates (`https://affiliate-program.amazon.com/`): Perfect for beginners; promote almost anything on Amazon.

  CJ Affiliate (`www.cj.com`): A major network with large, established brands.

2. E-Commerce & Dropshipping: The Modern Storefront

The world shops online. E-commerce allows you to sell physical products directly to a global audience.

- **The Traditional Model:** You create your own brand, source or manufacture products, and handle inventory and shipping using platforms like **Shopify** (`www.shopify.com`) or **Amazon FBA** (Fulfillment by Amazon) (`https://sellercentral.amazon.com`).
- **The Dropshipping Model:** A lower-risk entry point. You partner with a supplier (e.g., via **Oberlo** (`www.oberlo.com`) or **AliDropship** (`alidropship.com`)) who holds the inventory and ships products directly to your customer when you make a sale. You focus entirely on marketing and customer service.

3. The Creator Economy: Monetizing Your Expertise and Influence

This broad category revolves around building a personal or niche brand and monetizing your knowledge, skills, or personality.

- **Skills & Expertise Marketing (Knowledge Commerce):** Package your skills into sellable digital products.

  How it Works: Create online courses, webinars, or paid newsletters. Use platforms like **Teachable** or **Kajabi** to host your content, and tools like **GoToMeeting** (`www.gotomeeting.com`) or **Camtasia** (`www.techsmith.com/camtasia.html`) for creation.

- **Video Marketing & Personal Branding (YouTube, etc.):** Build a loyal following by creating valuable or entertaining video content.

  Revenue Streams: Ad revenue (via **Google AdSense**), brand sponsorships, affiliate marketing, and selling your own products. Platforms like **YouTube** (`www.youtube.com`) and **Vimeo** (`https://vimeo.com`) are your stage.

- **Freelancing & The Gig Economy:** Offer your specific skills on a project basis. This is the ultimate "skills-based economy."

  In-Demand Skills: Graphic design, writing, programming, digital marketing, virtual assistance.

  Top Platforms: Upwork (`www.upwork.com`), **Fiverr** (`www.fiverr.com`), **Toptal** (`www.toptal.com`), and **Freelancer** (`www.freelancer.com`).

4. The Tech Frontier: Software and Digital Products

If you have a unique idea for an app, software tool, or even a sophisticated digital template, you can bring it to life.

- **The Path:** You don't need to be a coder. Use freelance platforms like **Upwork** or **Toptal** to hire a developer. The key is identifying an unsolved problem or a need in the market and creating a digital solution.

Part 2: The Changing World of Work: Why These Skills Are Future-Proof

The urgency to build an online income is not just about opportunity, it's about necessity. The world of work is being reshaped by two powerful forces: **automation** and **global connectivity**.

The Automation Revolution: By 2030, roles centered on repetitive, predictable tasks are at high risk. Careers like cashiers, data entry clerks, telemarketers, and even some production and legal support roles are being rapidly automated.

The Rise of the Digital Native: The future favors skills that machines cannot easily replicate: creativity, strategic thinking, emotional intelligence, and digital literacy.

The Paradigm Shift:

The Industrial-Age Model	The Digital-Age Model
Working a 9-5 in a corporate office	Setting your own hours, working remotely
Following corporate hierarchy & politics	Leading your own projects and brand
Dependent on a single employer	Diversified income through multiple clients/streams
Static, company-provided training	Continuous, self-directed learning

Conclusion: Your Path Forward

The digital economy is not a passing trend; it is the foundation of our economic future. The choice is yours: be a passive observer of these changes, or actively participate and build your place within them.

Your journey starts now:

1. **Define Your "Why."**
2. **Choose one model** that aligns with your skills and interests.
3. **Commit to Learning.** The digital world evolves fast. Use platforms like **Udemy** (`www.udemy.com`), **Coursera** (`www.coursera.org`), and **Skillshare** (`www.skillshare.com`) to continuously upgrade your skills.
4. **Develop a simple plan and take action.**

   The individuals who will thrive are those who are adaptable, skilled, and aware. Don't let the future make you an afterthought. Equip yourself with the knowledge to not just survive, but to prosper in the 21st century and beyond.

Chapter 32

The Loyalty Loop

Mastering Customer Retention

& Strategic Email Marketing

The Foundation: Your Customer is Your Business

Every enduring business is built upon a single, indispensable asset: its customers. They are not merely revenue sources; they are the lifeblood, the validation of your purpose, and the partners in your growth. A company without a loyal customer base is an entity without a future. intelligent businesses recognize this profound value, continuously refining their offerings not just to meet, but to anticipate and elevate the lives of those they serve. In this paradigm, **the customer is not just king; they are the keystone of your entire enterprise.**

For new entrepreneurs, this truth is paramount. Your first customers are investing more than money, they are investing trust in your vision. Honoring that trust by delivering exceptional value is the non-negotiable first step toward sustainability.

Know Your Customer: The Strategic Inquiry

To build loyalty, you must move beyond assumptions and cultivate deep understanding. Begin by asking:

- **The Emotional Driver:** What truly delights your customers? Is it saving time, achieving status, gaining peace of mind, or experiencing joy?
- **The Problem Lens:** What persistent challenges or "**pain points**" do they face that your product or service can uniquely resolve?
- **The Value Equation:** How does your offering tangibly improve their daily life or business operations? Does the perceived value significantly outweigh the cost?
- **The Accessibility Check:** Is your pricing structured in a way that aligns with the value delivered and remains within their perceived affordability?

The Five Pillars of Enduring Relevance

To not only attract but permanently retain customers in a competitive market, you must excel in these five core areas:

1. Strategic Value Positioning (Beyond Just Price)
While competitive pricing is crucial, it's only one component of value. Customers seek the best *overall* deal, a combination of price, quality, and service. Instead of racing to the bottom, focus on **Value Transparency**. Justify your price through superior quality, warranty, customer service, or ethical sourcing. Use tools like **PriceGrid** or **Competitor Monitor** to track the market, but compete on value proposition, not just digits.

2. Curated Choice & Personalization
A vast selection is less important than a *relevant* selection. Use customer data to curate options that speak to different segments (e.g., **"premium," "essential," "budget-friendly"**). This simplifies decision-making and enhances the experience. Platforms like **Nosto** or **Adobe Commerce** offer powerful personalization engines that can recommend products dynamically, making each customer feel understood.

3. Uncompromising Quality & Consistency
Quality is the bedrock of trust and the primary justification for premium pricing. It's the reason customers choose Nike for performance durability or Patagonia for sustainable integrity. Implement rigorous Quality Assurance (QA) processes and actively solicit feedback through platforms like **Trustpilot** or **Yotpo**. Showcase your commitment to quality in your storytelling, it builds emotional equity.

4. Frictionless Convenience
Modern convenience means minimizing the effort a customer must expend. This includes:

- **User Experience (UX):** A seamless, intuitive website (test tools: **Hotjar**, **Crazy Egg**).
- **Logistics:** Fast, affordable, and transparent shipping (partners like **ShipStation** can help).
- **Accessibility:** Multiple service channels (chatbot, email, phone) with consistent information.
- **Simplification:** One-click purchasing, saved profiles, and easy returns.

Study leaders like **Amazon** (logistics), **Zappos** (service), and **Duolingo** (gamified engagement) to understand how they remove friction at every touchpoint.

5. Personalized Recognition & Experience
Personalization is the ultimate expression of customer-centricity. It moves from **"Here's what we sell" to "Here's what we know you'll love."** This can range from simple (using a first name in emails) to complex (custom product proposals based on past purchases). CRM tools like **HubSpot** or **Salesforce** are essential for tracking customer interactions and enabling meaningful personalization at scale.

Closing the Loop: Mastering these five pillars creates a **"Loyalty Loop"** where satisfied customers return, advocate, and provide the feedback needed to improve further.

Part 2: Email Mastery – The Art of Strategic Engagement

In an era of social noise, email remains the most direct, personal, and high-ROI marketing channel. But its effectiveness hinges on one critical skill: **getting it right the first time.**

The Modern Email Framework

Think of an email in two acts:

- **The Subject Line:** Its *sole* purpose is to earn the **open**. It is a promise, a spark of curiosity, or a solution to a nagging problem.
- **The Body:** Its purpose is to **deliver on that promise** with valuable content, building trust and guiding the reader toward a single, clear Call to Action (CTA).

Frequency & Rhythm: Be a Welcome Guest, Not an Intruder

Your sending schedule should match your content's value and your audience's expectations.

- **Daily:** For timely, subscription-style content (e.g., news digests, educational tips).
- **Weekly:** Ideal for most businesses—a consistent rhythm for newsletters, highlights, and promotions.
- **Monthly:** Best for deep-dive content, company updates, or curated resource roundups. Tools like **Mailchimp** or **ActiveCampaign** offer send-time optimization features to maximize open rates.

The Critical Mistake: Selling in the Subject Line

The fastest way to trigger a delete is to lead with a blatant sales pitch. The subject line is the invitation to the conversation, not the closing argument. Focus on **benefit** or **intrigue**, not the transaction.

The 11 Proven Subject Line Archetypes (With Modern Twists)

Here are timeless frameworks, updated for today's inbox:

1. **The FOMO (Fear of Missing Out):** Leverages scarcity and urgency.

   Example: "Your reservation expires tonight: [Product Name] back in stock."

2. **The Vanity/Status Appeal:** Taps into the desire for self-improvement or trend-setting.

   Example: "The [Industry] secret top performers won't talk about."

3. **The Direct Command:** Creates immediate clarity and action.

   Example: "Your guide to [Achievable Goal] is inside."

4. **The Pain Point Agitator:** Identifies a problem your reader feels deeply.

   Example: "Tired of [Universal Frustration]? Here's a different way."

5. **The "How-To" Solution:** Positions you as the helpful guide.

   Example: "How to [Desired Outcome] without [Common Obstacle]."

6. **The Mistake Revealer:** Offers to save the reader from error.

   Example: "The #1 mistake people make when choosing [Product Category]."

7. **The Secret-Sharer:** Builds intrigue and insider status.

   Example: "What the most successful [Your Client Type] do differently."

8. **The Fast Path:** Appeals to the desire for efficiency.

   Example: "A quicker way to [Time-Consuming Task]."

9. **The Curious Gap:** Poses a compelling, open-ended question.

   Example: "Is your [Something They Care About] actually working?"

10. **The Storyteller:** Uses personal narrative to build connection.

    Example: "How I went from [Starting Point] to [Desirable Result]."

11. **The Personalization Token:** Uses data to show relevance.

    Example: "For [Customer Name]: a thought on [Their Last Purchase/Interest]."

Mastering the Email Body

Once opened, your email must deliver value swiftly. Structure it with:

- **A Warm, Relevant Opening:** Acknowledge the subject line's promise.
- **High-Value Content:** Offer genuine insight, a useful tip, or an entertaining story.
- **Clear, Singular CTA:** Use a prominent button or link for the desired next step (e.g., "Read the full guide," "Claim your spot," "Shop the collection").
- **Clean Design & Mobile Optimization:** Over 50% of emails are opened on mobile. Test with tools like **Litmus**.

Continuous Improvement: The Key to Mastery

Email marketing is a science of testing. Use A/B testing (on subject lines, CTAs, send times) relentlessly. Resources like **Really Good Emails** for inspiration and **Send Check** for technical deliverability analysis are invaluable.

Creation: The Loyalty-Marketing Collaboration

Your customer retention strategy and your email marketing are intrinsically linked. The five pillars give you something *worth* communicating about, exceptional value, quality, and service. Email mastery provides the **direct, personalized channel** to communicate that value, nurture relationships, and invite customers back into the Loyalty Loop.

By excelling in both, you build a business that doesn't just attract customers, but creates devoted advocates for years to come.

Dear Reader,

Thank you for picking up ***The Digital World Playbook*** and investing your time and attention in its pages. Whether you're a seasoned professional navigating the digital landscape or someone just beginning to explore its vast potential, your curiosity and willingness to learn are what drive meaningful progress in our ever-evolving world.

Writing this book was an exercise in development and hope that we might better understand the tools and technologies shaping our lives and, in doing so, use them more intentionally, ethically, and effectively. Your engagement turns that hope into a shared journey. Knowing that these ideas are now in your hands, to be reflected upon, debated, or put into practice, is the greatest reward I could ask for as an author.

In a digital age often characterized by noise and distraction, your choice to read, reflect, and thoughtfully engage with these concepts is a powerful statement. It reaffirms that, despite the pace of change, human curiosity and the desire for meaningful connection remain at the heart of progress.

If anything within these pages has sparked a new idea, offered a useful strategy, or even prompted a moment of clarity, then this endeavor has been a success. I am deeply grateful to have you as part of this conversation.

With sincere appreciation,
Sterlyn Smith

www.ingramcontent.com/pod-product-compliance
Lightning Source LLC
LaVergne TN
LVHW061247100826
845148LV00008B/1054

* 9 7 8 1 7 3 5 2 9 4 2 7 8 *